FRENCH CUISINE

COOKING TO DINE

FRENCH CUISINE

Easy and elegant entertaining

Linda Gassenheimer

W. Foulsham & Co.Ltd.

London · New York · Toronto · Cape Town · Sydney

Design: Robert Mathias
Photographs: Mike O'Neill
Acknowledgements: Props for the
photographs: from Harrods, Souleido, Skye
Ceramics, Slough Ceramics, Wainwright and
Daughter, Truffles at Wainwright and
Daughter. Help with the photographs: Alberta
Strage, Alan and Anne Gordon, Mrs Deutsch,
Karen Reiseborough.

Dedication
For Harold whose patience and palette
supported my efforts to create this book

Cover Photograph: Poulet aux Champignons

W. Foulsham & Company Limited
Yeovil Road, Slough, Berkshire, SL1 4JH

ISBN 0–572–01273–X

Copyright © 1984 Linda Gassenheimer

Photoset in Great Britain by Input Typesetting
Ltd, London
and printed in Hong Kong

*Cold Buffet: (clockwise) Mousse aux Avocats (p 24),
Bavarois aux Framboises (p 134), Poire Vinaigrette (p 47),
Veau à l'Orange (p 94), Crudités (p 16), Terrine de Foie
de Porc (p 28)*

CONTENTS

INTRODUCTION

France is a beautiful and varied country. Driving through the countryside, one marvels at the rich farm land that stretches for miles and yields some of the world's best produce; and at the peaceful, well-manicured vineyards which belie the fact that some of the world's most superb wines are produced there. Bordered by water north, south and west, the Alps and Pyrenees, and with fertile river valleys throughout the land, France abounds in natural wealth. With this diverse geography producing an infinite array of natural food resources and a dedication to excellence characteristic of the culture, is it any wonder that France over the centuries has developed an exceptional, unique cuisine.

My love of simple, delicious food, beautifully served, was heightened during the years that I lived in Paris. A very sophisticated method of distribution means that fresh ingredients arrive at your table still in perfect condition. Home cooking or *cuisine de la famille* produces some of the best meals I have ever tasted. Roasting a chicken in the oven and simply adding water to the natural juices creates a dish fit for any gourmet. It is this outstanding quality of the fresh produce that forms the base of good French cuisine. The smell of fresh bread baked twice a day on the premises of each corner boulangerie stimulates anyone to create a meal to go with it. Waking up to the sound of our little boy returning home from the baker shouting, 'Hurry up, the croissants are still warm,' is a delight at the beginning of every day. Or going into the cheese shop and being asked, not on what day you wish to eat the cheese, but at what time today you need it, emphasises the extent of perfectionism that creates such superb results.

I have written this book for everyone who enjoys haute cuisine, but thinks they don't have the time or knowledge to prepare it at home. The recipes are simple, elegant and emphasise fundamental cooking techniques. Enjoying a meal that is simple, delicious and beautifully presented is a treat. This book is dedicated to achieving this art form. It does so by encouraging the user to take the very freshest of produce and prepare it to perfection so that all the natural flavours prevail.

An unusual feature is that nearly every recipe in the book can be prepared in advance up to a point, and many can be completely prepared in advance without sacrificing quality. This is a marvellous aid to the home chef. Each recipe describes what can be done in advance.

The use of the food processor has had a significant impact on French cuisine. Many dishes that were considered too much bother for the home table become easy and fun with these magical wonders. I have mentioned how you might use one to speed up your result.

The recipes have been selected and developed to present unusual and interesting dishes. We have all had a *Quiche Lorraine*, but what about a *Quiche Fantaisie* with a creamy mushroom base accentuated by fresh tarragon and thyme; or a creamy ham tart with the tang of calvados (which gives it the name *Tarte Normande*) and crème fraîche. I have also catered for chocolate lovers who may be surprised to find their favourite ambrosia in a sauce for duck.

The dessert section contains an appealing light chocolate mousse, made without egg yolks or cream. It is like biting into a chocolate cloud. The delicious chocolate flavour is centre stage here, and also in a chocolate cake made without flour. Chocolate first conquered the Indians of Central and South America and spread to all of us who can't resist its taste.

If you prefer the fresh, fruity, flavour of orange, this delectable citrus fruit is featured in a tangy tomato and orange soup. Oranges are used again to create a lovely light sauce to use with veal. I have also included several orange-based delights, which can proudly grace any dessert table.

The recipes have all been used and tested by my students at *CuisinEase*, my cookery dem-onstration centre, and you will find they can be produced with ease and elegance at home.

With the emphasis on bringing out the natural flavours in your dishes, the quality of the ingredients will be important to your success. Thus, I have given pointers on what to look for when shopping.

Even with the fast pace of our lives today, we can still explore and enjoy a passion for excellent cuisine in our own homes. With this in mind I have developed a type of recipe that meets all of my criteria of excellence, but leaves time for the pursuit of other interests. *Cooking to Dine* is the result of my search and I wish you and your guests, 'Bon Appetit'.

Linda Gassenheimer

AUTHOR'S NOTES

The recipes have been set out in an easy-to-follow pattern with special hints set apart. These hints have been included to help you understand why certain techniques and methods work. The aim is for you to be able to transfer this knowledge to other recipes using similar methods.

1. Measurements have been given in Metric, Imperial, and American equivalents. They are based on the use of English ingredients so if you use these recipes in other countries, allowances should be made for differences in ingredients in these areas.

2. Measurements for salt and pepper are very individual and vary according to taste. Unless an unusual amount is called for, the recipes say, 'Add salt and pepper to taste'. I use very little salt and recommend you do the same. Allow yourself to experience natural flavours and fresh herbs as used in the recipes. Start out with a pinch of seasoning and then add more only if necessary.

3. Basic recipes, such as for pastry, crêpes and vinaigrette, are included at the beginning of the section concerned. Techniques and hints, on the other hand, are repeated each time they are called for so that no referring back will be necessary.

4. Learning to sweat onions, or any member of the onion family, before adding other ingredients is important. This process takes away any bitter flavour the onions might have and brings out their natural sweetness. Also, it helps prevent curdling when milk or cream is to be added. This method is quite simple, enables you to do something else while the onions are cooking, and makes a world of difference in the results. See the glossary for the correct method.

5. Although butter has been specified in each of the recipes, margarine can, with only a few exceptions, be used equally well. I prefer to use butter with fish and egg recipes and when used in conjunction with chocolate.

6. In general, recipes that call for food to be served cold, really mean serve at room temperature. Food served directly out of the refrigerator does not have as much flavour.

7. Many recipes call for food to simmer at a low temperature. If your hob is not reliable at a low heat, use your oven at about 170°C/325°F/gas mark 3. Oven cooking tends to be drier than using a hob, so I place a piece of greaseproof paper over the food and then a lid to help keep in the moisture.

8. When a recipe calls for a certain amount of pastry, this means the amount of flour used, not what the pastry weighs when made. Thus 225 g/8 oz/1 cup of pâte brisée means pastry made with 225 g/8 oz/1 cup flour.

10

GLOSSARY AND SPECIAL TECHNIQUES

Bain Marie
A large tin or pan of hot water in which a smaller pan is placed for cooking contents.

Baking blind
This is the method used to bake a pastry shell without a filling. Place some tissue paper or greaseproof paper in a pastry-lined tin. Fill it with dried beans, rice, dried bread crusts, or anything that will weight down the paper. There are metal and ceramic beads made specially for this purpose. Half-way through the baking, remove the filling and paper and let the crust finish cooking. If not weighted, and left on its own the pastry will bubble and lose its shape.

Beating egg whites
Egg whites should be beaten at room temperature in a grease-free bowl. They will weep and lose their fullness if left in a bowl for any length of time; so beat up your whites and use them immediately. Whipping the whites in a copper bowl will give you one third more volume. The copper also stabilises the whites so they will hold their shape and will not weep, if properly beaten. Some recipes call for a pinch of cream of tartar to help stabilise the whites.

Bouquet Garni
This is a bundle of fresh herbs that is used to flavour various dishes. It consists of parsley, bay leaf and thyme. Usually several parsley stalks, a few branches of thyme and one bay leaf are tied together with kitchen string. These herbs are available throughout the year and are far better than using a ready-prepared bouquet garni. Sometimes a recipe will call for a bouquet garni with fennel, celery, leeks, or other vegetables or herbs, such as chevil, basil or tarragon. This means that the base of parsley, thyme and bay leaf should be used plus whatever other ingredient is called for.

Caramel
Caramel literally means burnt sugar. There are some general rules about making caramel.

1. The sugar must be completely dissolved in the water before the water is brought to the boil. If the water boils before it is clear, the granules of sugar will burn and lump and ruin your caramel.
2. Try not to stir the caramel. Gently shake the pan. If the sugar washes up the side of the pan, brush it down with a brush dipped in cold water.
3. Caramel can be made simply by placing sugar in a pan and melting it, although this can be tricky, and I recommend following the recipes given.

Chiffonade
A garnish made with shredded lettuce, sorrel or spinach. Used to decorate soups or cold dishes.

Crème fraîche
This is the natural fresh cream one finds in France. It is a heavy cream that is matured with natural ferments. It adds a wonderful flavour and texture to soups and sauces and is not to be confused with fresh sweet cream. It is now available in most delicatessens but a substitute is easy to make and gives excellent results if you cannot buy it locally.

To make crème fraîche
Use equal amounts of soured cream and double cream. Mix these two creams together and leave covered at room temperature for 8–12 hours. It will become thick. Place in the refrigerator. It is at its best about 36 hours after it is made. It will keep for about 8 days in the refrigerator

depending on the freshness of the cream used.

Deglazing

This is a method where liquid (either stock, wine or cream) is used to dilute the concentrated residues left in a pan where meat, fish, game or poultry has been cooked.

Fromage blanc

This is a low fat cheese used in French cooking. It may be bought with from nought to 40 per cent fat. A very good substitute can be made.

To make fromage blanc

Cottage cheese	225 g	8 oz	1 cup
Plain yogurt	250 g	9 oz	1 cup + 1 tbsp
Lemon juice	15 ml	1 tbsp	1 tbsp

Mix all these ingredients together in a food processor or liquidiser.

Gelatine

Powdered gelatine is protein extracted from animal bones and connective tissue. It should be sprinkled onto cold liquid and then gently warmed, or a hot liquid poured over it. It must first be blended with cold water to soften and wet the crystals. If it is boiled or brought above 82°C/180°F, there is a danger of the gelatine losing its gelling properties. Some ingredients such as too much sugar, fresh pineapple, or fresh kiwi inhibit the gelling process.

Half whip

Whip the cream until it is thick, and just barely holds its shape.

Julienne strips

These are vegetables cut into strips the size of thick matchsticks.

Melting chocolate

This is a complex subject. Chocolate can be very temperamental. Here are some general rules:

1. The chocolate must be kept dry. Do not let any steam or liquid mix in while melting. Alternatively, if a recipe calls for melting the chocolate with a liquid, then use the exact amount called for. The liquid must be at least one tablespoon.

2. The easiest way to melt chocolate is to place it in a covered pan over boiling water. Immediately turn off the heat under the water and let it sit until melted.

3. Chocolate melts beautifully in a microwave oven. Follow the instructions for your particular oven.

4. If the chocolate seizes up when melting, then a small amount of vegetable oil can be added.

Panade

Thick sauce made like a roux or like choux pastry, used to bind ingredients.

Quenelles

Light savoury rolls, soufflé-like in texture, made from meat or fish.

Roux

This is the thickening element in sauces and soups. It is a mixture of a fatty element, usually butter or margarine, and flour. There are three basic kinds of roux: white roux, blond roux and brown roux. White roux consists of cooking the flour and fat together so that it remains white before a liquid is added. In a blond roux, cook the flour and fat until it is a straw colour before the liquid is added. The flour in a brown roux is cooked to a russet brown before addition of the liquid. These are the bases of all major French sauces.

Scald

Heat milk to just below boiling point, when small bubbles start to appear at the sides of the pan.

Sweating onions

Learning to sweat onions, or any member of the onion family, before adding other ingredients is important. This process takes away any bitter flavour the onions might have and brings out their natural sweetness. Also, it helps prevent curdling when milk or cream is added. Place the sliced or chopped onions in a pan with some melted butter, or a combination of fat and oil, and gently sauté them for about a minute. Then add a small amount of water to the onions, and place a piece of greaseproof paper on top to cover the pan. Place a tight-fitting lid over the top and lower the heat. Let the onions steam in this way for about 5–10 minutes until they are transparent. Take the lid off and continue to sauté to let all the moisture evaporate. This method is quite simple, enables you to do something else while the onions are cooking, and makes a world of difference in the results.

Truss

To tie a bird into a compact shape before cooking.

LES ENTRÉES
FIRST COURSES

First courses are very often my favourite part of the meal. They should be light and tasty and whet one's appetite for things to come. I have included a wide range to choose from, and hope you will find several that will please you. If you do choose one that is very filling, then the rest of the meal should be very light. Many starters make excellent luncheon dishes or light supper dishes.

Hints on Choosing and Serving your First Course

If you are having a formal and somewhat elaborate dinner, then it is a good idea to start with a cold dish. Heating too many things in the kitchen when serving a lot of people can lead to disaster. A first course sitting at each place as the guests enter the room is very pretty and makes the serving much easier. A French chef once told me that when he serves at home, he never has more than one hot course. He feels that he and his guests enjoy themselves more when he doesn't spend the entire meal in the kitchen.

Try to choose a first course that complements the rest of the meal. Repetition of the same ingredients is uninteresting. Thus, if oranges are in season don't use them in each course. Equally, if you serve a tart or crêpes, don't use a pastry base for your dessert. A well balanced choice produces the most desirable effect.

It's a good idea to work with food that is in season. You will have better results and it won't cost the earth to achieve them. If you have a favourite recipe that always works but the ingredients are difficult to find in winter then wait until spring to use it. In addition, your guests are more likely to appreciate a hot soup or onion tart in the winter, while a special salad or vegetable would be a summer treat.

COUPE AUX TOMATES ET AUX ORANGES
Tomato and Orange Coupe

This dish creates a pretty picture for your table, especially when served in small glass dishes so that the colours can be seen. It can be made in advance and placed on the table before your guests arrive, or it can be served on one platter as a salad or attractive buffet dish. The dressing is very good on other salads.

Preparation time: 20 minutes To serve: 6

INGREDIENTS	METRIC	IMPERIAL	AMERICAN
Oranges	5	5	5
Firm tomatoes	6	6	6
FOR THE TOMATO SAUCE: (TO MAKE 225 ml/8 oz/1 CUP SAUCE)			
Onion, chopped	1 med	1 med	1 med
Butter	25 g	1 oz	2 tbsp
Garlic, crushed	1 clove	1 clove	1 clove
Ripe tomatoes, quartered	450 g	1 lb	1 lb
Salt and freshly ground black pepper to taste			
Large pinch of sugar			
Bouquet garni (1 bay leaf, 2 branches thyme, several parsley stalks, all tied together.)			
Tomato purée (paste) (optional)	5 g	1 tsp	1 tsp
Salt and freshly ground black pepper			

FOR THE DRESSING:

Red wine vinegar	25 ml	2 tbsp	2 tbsp
Vegetable oil	85 ml	6 tbsp	6 tbsp
Lemon juice (optional)			
Chopped herbs (tarragon, parsley, chives, fresh if possible)	25 g	2 tbsp	2 tbsp

To make the tomato sauce

Sweat the onions in the butter until they are transparent. Add the garlic, then the tomatoes and bouquet garni. Cover and simmer for about 10 minutes. The tomatoes will cook to a sauce. If your tomatoes are not ripe it may take longer. Remove the bouquet garni. Purée the mixture in a food processor, or put through a food mill, or simply sieve. If it is still quite liquid, place back on the heat to reduce. It should have the consistency of thick tomato sauce. Add salt and pepper to taste. Add the sugar (tomatoes contain a lot of acid and need a little sweetener). Taste and correct seasoning if necessary.

This sauce may be made in advance and stored in the refrigerator. If using winter tomatoes, you may wish to add tomato purée to taste, for colour and flavour.

To prepare the oranges and tomatoes

Peel the oranges. With a serrated knife cut underneath the skin of the orange and with a sawing motion cut off the skin, moving the orange round in a circle. Try to cut underneath the skin between the pith and flesh of the orange. Section the orange by cutting between the membrane and the flesh to the centre of the orange. Do this at every membrane. You will be left with segments that do not have pith or membrane.

To peel the tomatoes, place them one at a time in boiling water for 8–12 seconds. Immediately remove them to a bowl of iced water. This will stop the flesh under the skin becoming soft. The skin will easily peel off. Quarter the tomatoes (if they are large cut into six) and remove the seeds.

Coupe aux Tomates et aux Oranges

HINT: If you wish, serve the tomatoes unpeeled. Today's emphasis on wholesome food allows us to serve these dishes in a less formal way.

To finish the dressing

Add the vinegar and oil to the tomato sauce. Taste for seasoning. Add more salt, pepper or sugar as needed. If it needs more tartness, add a little lemon juice. Add the chopped herbs, saving a little to sprinkle on top.

To serve

Place the orange and tomato sections in each individual dish alternating them for a colourful effect. Use glass fruit dishes, small ramekins, or arrange the sections on small plates. Spoon the sauce over them. Sprinkle the remaining herbs on top.

15

CRUDITÉS
Raw Vegetable Starter

The French love a colourful display of raw vegetables cut in different shapes. It gives them an opportunity to show off their top quality produce and their delicate sauces. Usually crudités are served as a first course, but they may be offered as a salad course. Variety is important in successful crudités and, for that reason, a range of vegetables have been suggested. These recipes can be used together to form one platter or may be used as separate salads.

Preparation time: 30 minutes To serve: 6

CAROTTES RÂPÉES
Grated Carrots

INGREDIENTS	METRIC	IMPERIAL	AMERICAN
Carrots	225 g	½ lb	½ lb
Raisins	75 g	3 oz	¾ cup
Vinaigrette sauce (page 75)			

Wash and peel the carrots. Wash and dry the raisins. Grate the carrots either in the food processor or in a food mill fitted with a grating disc. Mix the raisins into the carrots and spoon some vinaigrette sauce over the top.

SALADE DE BETTERAVES
Beetroot Salad

	METRIC	IMPERIAL	AMERICAN
Medium beetroot (These may be bought already cooked or raw)	4–5	4–5	4–5
Vinaigrette sauce (page 75)			
Single (light) cream	25 ml	2 tbs	2 tbs

If the beetroot is raw, place in salted cold water, cover and bring to the boil. Cook until tender when pricked with the point of a knife (about 1½ hours). Take the skin off the beetroot and cut into small cubes. Make the basic vinaigrette sauce and add the cream. Pour over the beetroot.

SALADE DE CONCOMBRES
Cucumber Salad

INGREDIENTS	METRIC	IMPERIAL	AMERICAN
Cucumber	1 large	1 large	1 large
Salt	10 g	2 tsp	2 tsp
FOR THE DRESSING:			
Dill seeds	15 g	1 tbsp	1 tbsp
Boiling water	85 ml	3 fluid oz	6 tbsp
Sugar	15 g	1 tbsp	1 tbsp
White wine vinegar	50 ml	4 tbsp	4 tbsp
Salt and freshly ground black pepper to taste			
TO GARNISH:			
Fresh dill	15 g	1 tbsp	1 tbsp

Peel and thinly slice the cucumber.

HINT: To make an attractive green and white effect, wash the cucumber skin and peel the cucumber in alternate strips so that you are left with green and white stripes.

Place the slices in a collander and sprinkle with salt. Leave for at least 30 minutes. The salt will draw out the juices leaving the slices limp, but fresh tasting. Wash in cold water to remove the salt and drain.

To make the dressing
Press the dill seeds with a spoon to release their oils, and pour on the boiling water. Leave to infuse until the water is cool. Strain. Add the sugar, wine vinegar and salt and pepper to the water. Taste for seasoning.

To serve
Spoon the dressing over the cucumber slices. Sprinkle with fresh dill.

SALADE DE CHAMPIGNONS
Mushroom Salad

INGREDIENTS	METRIC	IMPERIAL	AMERICAN
Mushrooms	100 g	4 oz	1 cup
Fresh lemon juice	10 ml	2 tsp	2 tsp
Grape-seed or peanut oil	20 ml	1 ½ tbsp	1½ tbsp
Salt and freshly ground black pepper to taste			

Wash the mushrooms and cut them into medium slices.

> *HINT: Try not to get mushrooms very wet when cleaning them. The best method is to wipe them carefully with damp kitchen paper.*

To make the dressing
Mix the lemon juice and oil together and season.

Mix the mushrooms into the vinaigrette and leave to marinate for 5 minutes. Serve.

SALADE DE COURGETTES
Courgette Salad

INGREDIENTS	METRIC	IMPERIAL	AMERICAN
Courgettes (zucchini)	3 small	3 small	3 small
Vinaigrette sauce (page 75)			
FOR THE GARNISH:			
Fresh coriander leaves, chopped	15 g	1 tbsp	1 tbsp

Wash the courgettes and slice in julienne strips (thick matchsticks). This may be done in a food processor. Spoon the vinaigrette sauce over them and serve with chopped coriander leaves sprinkled over.

SALADE DE POIVRONS
Pepper Salad

INGREDIENTS	METRIC	IMPERIAL	AMERICAN
Green pepper	1	1	1
Red pepper	1	1	1
Yellow pepper	1	1	1
Vinaigrette sauce (page 75)			

Wash and de-seed the peppers. Slice in 5 cm/ 2 in strips. Place the strips in boiling water. As soon as the water returns to the boil, drain and refresh with cold water to stop the cooking and set the colour. Spoon the dressing over them and serve.

SALADE DE MAÏS
Sweetcorn salad

INGREDIENTS	METRIC	IMPERIAL	AMERICAN
Sweetcorn, canned or frozen	325 g	11½ oz	1½ cup
Sweet pimentos, canned	185 g	6.5 oz	¾ cup
Vinaigrette sauce (page 75)			
Onion, chopped	10 g	2 tsp	2 tsp
Single (light) cream	15 ml	1 tbsp	1 tbsp

(If good fresh corn is available, cook it and remove the kernels. If fresh red peppers are available, roast and skin and pour olive oil over them.)

Drain the sweetcorn and dice the pimentos. Mix together. Make the vinaigrette sauce, and add the onion and cream. Pour over the corn and mix well. Serve.

The list could be extended to any type of vegetable available to you. Try to select with variation of colour and texture in mind.

SALADE DE PRINTEMPS
Spring Salad

This is a salad made from the very freshest of greens and vegetables. The dressing is as light and fresh as the seasonal ingredients. Any type of vegetables can be substituted as long as they are of the best quality.

Preparation time: 30 minutes To serve: 6

INGREDIENTS	METRIC	IMPERIAL	AMERICAN
Small fresh green beans (If large ones are used, cut them in half lengthways).	225 g	½ lb	2 cups
Asparagus (Count on 3 per person.)	450 g	1 lb	1 lb
Lettuce (red batavia, romain, lambs' ears, Belgian endive or escarole, or any unusual types of lettuce. Choose a mixture if possible.)			
Smoked streaky bacon	100 g	4 oz	¼ lb
Walnut halves	100 g	4 oz	1 cup
FOR THE DRESSING:			
Lemon juice	10 ml	2 tsp	2 tsp
Peanut oil	20 ml	4 tsp	2 tsp
Olive oil	20 ml	4 tsp	4 tsp
Sherry wine vinegar	10 ml	2 tsp	2 tsp
Fresh chervil, chopped (If unavailable use fresh parsley mixed with a little tarragon.)	25 g	2 tbsp	2 tbsp
Salt and freshly ground black pepper to taste			

To prepare the vegetables
Top and tail the green beans. If they are young they will not need stringing. Peel the asparagus and break off the woody part of the butt end. Blanch these vegetables in separate pans by placing them in boiling water. Leave the green beans in the water for 2 minutes. Leave the asparagus for 6 minutes. When they are cooked, drain and refresh under cold water.

Break off enough lettuce leaves to give a base for 6 individual plates. If you are using several types, then 3–4 leaves of each type is enough.

HINT: To get a variation of colour and texture, break the head of lettuce in half and take some young leaves from the centre and older leaves from the outside.

Prepare the bacon
Place the strips of bacon on a rack over a baking tray or drip pan and place in the oven at 180°C/350°F gas mark 4 for 15–20 minutes until crisp. Drain on a kitchen towel and break into small pieces.

Prepare the walnuts
Place on a baking tray and roast in the same oven as for the bacon for 10 minutes.

For the dressing
Whisk the lemon juice and two oils together. Add the vinegar and herbs. Add salt and pepper to taste. Whisk well.

To assemble
Mix the beans and asparagus into the dressing. Arrange the lettuce leaves on the individual plates. Place the asparagus radiating out from the centre like the spokes of a wheel. Place the beans around the lettuce. Sprinkle with the nuts and bacon. Sprinkle any leftover dressing on the leaves.

Salade de Printemps

POIREAUX A LA VINAIGRETTE
Leeks Vinaigrette

Leeks make a wonderful winter salad as well as a delicious vegetable. If possible, use small baby leeks which are sweeter. However, any fresh leeks create a delicious dish.

Preparation time: 10 minutes To serve: 6

INGREDIENTS	METRIC	IMPERIAL	AMERICAN
Leeks	900 g	2 lb	2 lb
FOR THE VINAIGRETTE:			
Red wine vinegar	40 ml	3 tbsp	3 tbsp
Dijon mustard	15 ml	1 tbsp	1 tbsp
Corn or sunflower oil	150 ml	5 oz	½ cup + 1 tbsp
Fresh parsley, chopped	40 g	3 tbsp	3 tbsp
Salt and freshly ground black pepper to taste			

To prepare the leeks
Cut off the untidy green parts, and shave off the root at the bulb end of the leek. Try to leave some of the root intact so that the leek will keep its shape. Wash the leeks by standing the green end in a jug of cold water. Leave them in the water for 5 minutes. Remove and look to see if there are any dark spots under the first layers. If there are, make a small slit where the spot is and wash under running water. This way the leeks will be cleaned and left whole. Place the leeks lying down in a pot of salted boiling water. Cook uncovered for 10 minutes or until the leeks are tender. Carefully lift them out of the water and place on a rack in the sink. Let cold water run over them to stop the cooking and bring out their colour. Allow to drain.

To prepare the vinaigrette
While the leeks are cooking, make the vinaigrette. Pour the wine vinegar into a bowl and add the mustard. Whisk well to make sure they are thoroughly mixed. Add the oil and whisk.

HINT: The vinaigrette will be thick and creamy only if the vinegar and mustard are well mixed before the oil is added. If your kitchen is warm then make sure your oil is cold.

To finish
Gently squeeze any remaining water from the leeks and lay one layer in an oval serving dish. Pour a little of the vinaigrette over them. Lay another row of leeks on the first one starting about 12 mm/½ in from the end so that some of the white heads show from the previous row. Continue to layer the leeks, spooning a little vinaigrette on each row. End with a coating of vinaigrette on top and sprinkle with the reserved parsley. This may be made hours in advance and kept at room temperature.

To serve
Serve on individual plates as a first course or salad, or use for a buffet.

HINT: The vinaigrette should be poured over the leeks while they are still slightly warm. They will absorb more of the flavour this way.

MOUSSE DE POISSON FUMÉ
Smoked Haddock Mousse

This is a perfect cold buffet as well as first course dish. It can be made a day in advance and is very attractive to serve. Since it is rich, a little goes a long way.

Preparation time: 15–20 minutes To serve: 6–8

INGREDIENTS	METRIC	IMPERIAL	AMERICAN
Smoked haddock fillets	340 g	¾ lb	¾ lb
Milk or water to cover			
Gelatine	15 g	½ oz	1 tbsp
Chicken stock	70 ml	2½ oz	⅓ cup

Eggs, hard-boiled	2	2	2
Mayonnaise (page 75)	140 g	5 oz	½ cup + 1 tbsp
Double cream	70 ml	2½ oz	⅓ cup
Salt and freshly ground black pepper to taste			
TO GARNISH:			
Aspic jelly	600 ml	1 pt	2 ½ cups
Eggs, hard-boiled	2	2	2
Small sprig of parsley			

To poach the haddock

Place the haddock in a small frying pan and cover with water. Bring the water to the boil.

HINT: This step helps to reduce the salt content.

Drain the fish and place back in the pan. Cover with a mixture of milk and water or with milk only. Bring the liquid to the boil and take off the heat. Cover and let stand for 10 minutes. Take the fish out and pat dry. Flake with a fork, taking out any bones.

To dissolve the gelatine

Sprinkle the gelatine onto the chicken stock. Dissolve carefully over a low heat, or set in a pan and place over hot water.

HINT: The gelatine must dissolve completely. No grains should be left in the bottom of the pan. If you set it over hot water when you start the recipe, it should be dissolved by the time you need it. Be careful not to boil the gelatine; it will lose its gelling properties.

To make the mousse

Coarsely chop the eggs and add to the flaked fish. Mix well. This may be done in a food processor or passed through the medium sieve of a food mill. Add the mayonnaise. Add salt and pepper to taste. Be careful not to add too much salt as the smoked fish is already salty. Add the dissolved gelatine to the mixture. Half whip the cream so that it slightly holds its shape. Fold into the mixture. It will fold in better if it is nearly the same consistency as the fish. Turn into a soufflé dish. It can also be turned into individual ramekins or a shallow serving bowl. It should three-quarters fill the container. Cover with cling film. Place in the refrigerator to set. It can be made a day ahead up to here.

HINT: The mousse should be cold and set when the aspic is put on, or the fish oil will cloud the aspic.

To garnish

Dissolve the aspic according to the packet instructions. Bring it up to the boil stirring constantly. Let cool. It will be syrupy when ready.

HINT: It is best to place some of the aspic in a pan over ice. It should be slightly thick as you use it. If it becomes too thick, then place over the heat again. Work in this way until the decoration is complete.

Thinly slice the two hard boiled eggs and place on a plate. Spoon some aspic over the eggs and allow to set. This will seal the yolk and keep it from spoiling the rest of the aspic. Spoon a thin layer of aspic over the top of the mousse. Wait a few minutes for it to start to set. Carefully place the eggs in a circle around the top leaving about 12 mm/½ in space from the edge. Place a small sprig of parsley in the centre. Spoon the aspic over the decoration to seal. You should have no more than a 12 mm/½ in layer of aspic in all. Refrigerate until ready to use. Serve at room temperature.

HINT: Do not pour the aspic, spoon it gently over the food. If you pour, you will have bubbles forming which are very difficult to disperse.

To serve

Serve the mousse from its dish, scooping out each portion at the table. Or use as part of a buffet. If you have made the mousse in individual ramekins, serve as it is.

ROULADES DE JAMBON
Ham Roll-Ups with Special Salad

This is a pretty dish that will brighten up any table. The roll-ups can be made a day in advance and the salad made a few hours before serving. Melon forms a surprise flavour in the salad and the vinaigrette is flavoured with the sweet melon juice.

Preparation time: 15 minutes To serve: 6

INGREDIENTS	METRIC	IMPERIAL	AMERICAN
Smoked ham, in thin slices	12	12	12
FOR THE FILLING:			
Curd cheese	225 g	8 oz	½ lb
(Philadelphia cream cheese may be used)			
Walnuts, chopped	50 g	2 oz	½ cup
Smoked ham, chopped	100 g	4 oz	¼ lb
FOR THE SALAD GARNISH:			
Firm red tomatoes	450 g	1 lb	1 lb
Cucumber	½	½	½
Ripe melon	1	1	1
Parsley, chopped	25 g	2 tbsp	2 tbsp
Mint, chopped	25 g	2 tbsp	2 tbsp
FOR THE VINAIGRETTE:			
White wine vinegar	25 ml	2 tbsp	2 tbsp
Mustard	10 g	2 tsp	2 tsp
Corn or sunflower oil	85 ml	6 tbsp	6 tbsp
Salt and freshly ground black pepper to taste			

Roulades de Jambon

To make the filling
Soften the curd cheese. Add the walnuts and chopped ham. If the mixture is too firm add a little milk to loosen it. This may be done in the food processor.

To make the roll-ups
Place the sliced ham on a flat surface and place a small spoonful of the filling across one end. Roll up the ham and put it in a shallow bowl or loaf tin. Fill all the slices and place them packed tightly together so that they will keep their shape. Cover with cling film and chill.

To make the salad
Peel the tomatoes by placing them one at a time in boiling water for 8–12 seconds and plunge them immediately into cold water to keep the flesh underneath from cooking. Quarter or cut into sixths if they are large. Take out the seeds. Cut into bite-sized cubes. Peel the cucumber and slice in half lengthways. Take out the seeds. Cut into cubes about the same size as the tomatoes. Don't make the pieces too big.

Slice the melon in half and take out the seeds. Cut into cubes the same size as the others. Try to cut the melon over a bowl and catch the juices. Squeeze any juice you can from the skin and save.

To make the vinaigrette
Put the vinegar and mustard in a small bowl and whisk well. Add the oil, salt and pepper and whisk until creamy. Add the juice saved from the melon. Taste for seasoning. Mix into the salad.

To serve
Place the ham roll-ups on an oval serving dish. Spoon the salad over the roll-ups and sprinkle with the chopped herbs. The dish may also be served on individual dishes. Two roll-ups per serving is enough for a first course.

MOUSSE AUX AVOCATS
Avocado Mousse

This mousse is rich, therefore a little goes a long way. It looks pretty and colourful and is an attractive addition to a buffet table.

Preparation time: 20 minutes To serve: 10

INGREDIENTS	METRIC	IMPERIAL	AMERICAN
Gelatine	15 g	½ oz	1 tbsp
Chicken stock	150 ml	5 fl oz.	⅔ cup
Ripe avocados	2	2	2
Onion, finely chopped	10 g	2 tsp	2 tsp
Worcestershire sauce	15 ml	1 tbsp	1 tbsp
Juice of ½ lemon			
Salt and freshly ground black pepper to taste			
Mayonnaise (page 75)	150 ml	5 oz	⅔ cup
Double or whipping (heavy) cream	150 ml	5 oz	⅔ cup
TO GARNISH:			
Red and Green Pepper Salad (page 25)			

You will need a 850 ml/1½ pint/3¾ cup mould. One with a circle cut out of the middle, makes the mousse look attractive.

Lightly oil the mould by dipping your finger in some oil and rubbing it over the mould. There should be a satiny finish with no drops of oil showing.

To dissolve the gelatine
Sprinkle the gelatine onto the chicken stock. Dissolve carefully over a low heat or in a pan over hot water.

HINT: The gelatine must dissolve completely. No grains should be left in the bottom of the pan. If you set it over hot water when you start the recipe, it should be dissolved by the time you need it. Be careful not to boil the gelatine; it will lose its gelling properties.

To make the mousse
Mash the avocados. Add the onion, Worcestershire sauce, lemon, salt and pepper. This may be done in a food processor. Taste for seasoning and add more if needed. Pour the dissolved gelatine onto the mixture. Fold the mayonnaise into the mixture. Half whip the cream.

HINT: When folding one mixture into another, the two should be of the same consistency. They will combine more easily this way. Thus, the cream should just be holding its shape but not firm.

Fold the cream into the mixture. Pour into the mould. Place a piece of oiled greaseproof paper over the top to help prevent the avocado from turning dark. Cover with cling film and place in the refrigerator to set.

To finish
Unmould onto a round serving platter. To do this, first loosen the edges of the mousse with a knife. Then quickly immerse the entire mousse in a sink filled with warm water. This includes the top. Dry the top with kitchen towel and unmould. You are trying to loosen the air lock that forms when the mousse is poured in.

HINT: It is a good idea to moisten the platter before unmoulding: this will allow you to slide the mould to the centre, if necessary. It is very frustrating to unmould something on the side of the platter and find that you can't get it into the centre.

Fill the centre hole with the Red and Green Pepper Salad and spoon the rest around the sides.

To serve
Slice the mousse and serve individual portions with some of the salad.

SALADE AUX DEUX POIVRONS

Red and Green Pepper Salad

INGREDIENTS	METRIC	IMPERIAL	AMERICAN
Green peppers	2	2	2
Red peppers	1	1	1
Prawns	50 g	2 oz	½ cup
Vinaigrette (Page 75)	40 ml	3 tbsp	3 tbsp
Black or green olives	6	6	6

Cut the peppers in half and take out the seeds. Slice the peppers into strips about 4 cm/1½ in long and 1.2 cm/½ in wide. Blanch them by placing them in boiling water and draining as soon as the water comes back to the boil. Refresh in cold water. Mix the peppers and prawns with the vinaigrette. Add the olives.

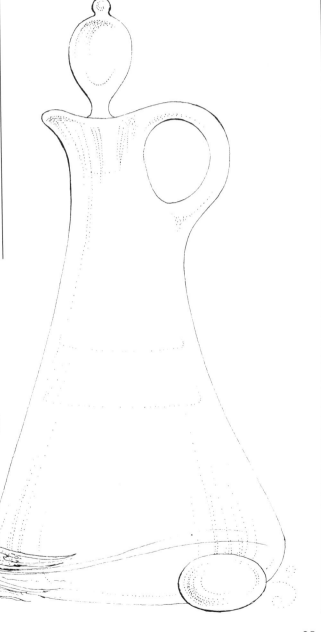

ASPIC DE SAUMON ET DE CONCOMBRE

Salmon and Cucumber in Aspic

This is a very colourful and light pâté, held together by aspic rather than meat or pork fat. I enjoy serving this dish in the spring as it captures the freshness of the season. It is pretty to serve and can be made well ahead.

Preparation time: 35 minutes To serve: 6

INGREDIENTS	METRIC	IMPERIAL	AMERICAN
Salmon fillet (salmon trout may be used)	450 g	1 lb	1 lb
FOR THE COURT BOUILLON TO POACH THE SALMON:			
White wine	225 ml	8 fl oz	1 cup
Water	225 ml	8 fl oz	1 cup
Carrot, sliced	1 small	1 small	1 small
Onion, sliced	1 small	1 small	1 small
Bouquet garni (1 bay leaf, parsley stalks, 1 branch thyme, all tied together)			
Hard-boiled eggs, coarsely chopped	2	2	2
1 packet aspic (enough to make 600 ml/20 fl oz/2½ cups aspic)			
White wine or madeira	25 ml	2 tbsp	2 tbsp
Cucumber cut into thick julienne or matchsticks	1	1	1
Fresh parsley, chopped	25 g	2 tbsp	2 tbsp
Fresh tarragon, chopped	25 g	2 tbsp	2 tbsp
Fresh chervil, chopped	25 g	1 tbsp	1 tbsp
1 small can pimentos sliced in julienne strips	100 g	4 oz	1 cup
Drained green peppercorns	15 g	1 tbsp	1 tbsp
Terrine, or loaf tin	2.2 l	2 quart	10 cups

To poach the fish:

Simmer all the ingredients for the court bouillon for about half an hour. Poach the salmon in the bouillon for about 2–3 minutes. Remove the salmon and discard any bones that remain. Pat dry with kitchen paper and cut into thick strips.

While the fish is cooling prepare the aspic according to the packet instructions. Do not bring it to the boil. Add the white wine or madeira. Leave to cool.

To fill the terrine:

Place the terrine in a bowl or pan of cold water and ice. It will be easier to work over the iced water. Spoon a layer of the cooled aspic over the bottom of the pan 6 mm/¼ in thick. Wait until it begins to set then layer the salmon and cucumber on the setting aspic. Spoon in another thin layer of aspic and wait for it to start to set. Sprinkle in the eggs and fresh herbs, pimentos and peppercorns in a thin layer. Then spoon more aspic over the mixture. Continue in this manner, alternating layers. With each layer wait until the aspic is nearly setting before adding more ingredients. In this way the terrine will be filled with all the ingredients floating evenly throughout. The last layer should be one of aspic. Refrigerate to set.

To unmould:

First loosen the edges with a knife. Then quickly immerse the entire dish into a sink filled with warm water. This includes the top of the terrine. Dry the top with a kitchen towel and unmould. (You are trying to loosen the air lock that forms when the aspic is poured in).

HINT: It is a good idea to moisten the platter before unmoulding; this will allow you to slide the mould to the centre, if necessary. It is very frustrating to unmould something on the side of the platter and find that you can't get it into the centre.

To serve:

The dish can be unmoulded and served on a platter or it can be sliced from the terrine.

Aspic de Saumon et de Concombre

PÂTÉ DE FOIE DE VOLAILLE
Chicken Liver Pâté

One memorable lesson I had in France taught me that the French never throw anything away. My instructor made three courses out of one little chicken. She cut up the chicken to make a delicious and quick chicken in wine sauce; the carcass, neck, giblets, feet and even the head went into making a thick and nourishing soup, and the liver made a beautiful pâté. So don't throw away any of the nourishment offered by a chicken. If you buy two chickens, you will have enough liver to fill a ramekin and use it as an hors d'oeuvre or a first course. It freezes well. I usually have one in my freezer to serve with drinks if someone drops in.

Cooking time: 10 minutes To serve: 6

INGREDIENTS	METRIC	IMPERIAL	AMERICAN
Butter	75 g	3 oz	1/3 cup
Onion, chopped	1 med	1 med	1 med
Garlic, crushed	1 clove	1 clove	1 clove
Chicken livers	225 g	8 oz	8 oz
Fresh parsley, chopped	25 g	2 tbsp	2 tbsp
Bay leaf	1	1	1
Branches of thyme (leaves only)	2	2	2
Brandy	15 ml	1 tbsp	1 tbsp
Salt and freshly ground black pepper to taste			

Melt half the butter in a saucepan and sweat the onion until transparent. Add the garlic and cook for 1 minute. Add the chicken livers and sauté for 2–3 minutes. Break the bay leaf into small pieces and add to the livers while they are cooking.

HINT: Try not to overcook the livers. They should still be very juicy and not dried out.

Even if there are still some dark spots that have not fully been cooked, do not worry. Liver cooks so quickly that these will finish cooking in their own heat once removed from the heat.

Sprinkle with the herbs and salt and pepper and cook for a further minute. Chop well (chop in a food processor, pass the mixture through the fine sieve of a food mill, or chop on a board). Stir in the brandy and taste. Try not to over-power the flavour with too much brandy. Add more salt and pepper if necessary.

To finish
This can be done in several ways. The pâté can be packed into a mould and chilled, then un-moulded and served on a platter with fresh parsley to decorate. Or it can be packed into individual ramekins or one large one. If you intend to freeze it or even store it in a refrigerator to serve later, melt the remaining butter and pour it over the top to seal. Chill.

To serve
Serve with thin slices of toasted bread and butter.

TERRINE DE FOIE DE PORC
Pork Terrine

Terrines have been a traditional part of most cuisines for centuries. Long before the days of refrigeration it was the custom to have some 'meat' ready to serve at any time of the day or night in case travellers called in. Terrines were easily made and kept for at least two weeks without refrigeration. Today, even with our modern conveniences, a good terrine is much appreciated. They make wonderful first-course, luncheon or picnic dishes with very little effort on the part of the chef. The use of a terrine or earthenware dish is a help in this recipe. The terrine cools down slowly and this helps to add to the flavour of the dish. However, the dish can be made in a metal loaf tin if you do not have a proper terrine.

Cooking time: 50 minutes To serve: 6–8

INGREDIENTS	METRIC	IMPERIAL	AMERICAN
Pork liver, finely chopped	175 g	6 oz	6 oz
Pork belly or any type of pork, minced	340 g	12 oz	¾ lb
Sausage meat	75 g	3 oz	3 oz
Onion, chopped	1 small	1 small	1 small
Egg	1	1	1
Cognac	15 ml	1 tbsp	1 tbsp
Nutmeg	10 g	2 tsp	2 tsp
Salt and freshly ground pepper to taste			
Smoked streaky bacon	225 g	8 oz	½ lb
Branch of thyme	1	1	1
Bay leaf	1	1	1
Terrine with lid, measuring 18 cm/7 in × 11.5 cm/ 4½ in and 7.5 cm/3 in deep			

To prepare the meat
Ask your butcher to mince all the meat for you. If he can't, chop in a food processor or put through a meat mincer. Mix all the ingredients together, except the bacon, thyme and bay leaf. Season well. Taste by taking a small amount and sautéing it for a minute. It should be well seasoned. Add more seasoning if necessary. Let it rest in the refrigerator overnight.

To prepare the terrine
The next day, prepare the strips of bacon by cutting any rind or bones off them, laying them on a flat surface and scraping them with a knife. This will stretch them out. Then line the terrine. The strips will stick to the sides of the terrine quite easily.

To finish
Pre-heat the oven to 190°C/375°F/gas mark 5. Fill the terrine with the meat mixture. Cover the top with strips of bacon. Place the branch of thyme and bay leaf on top. Cover with a lid. Seal the cover to the base of the terrine by making a thick paste of equal quantities of flour and water. Spoon the paste into the crack between the lid and the base. Do not seal the little hole in the terrine lid as steam must escape from it. Place in a roasting pan and three-quarters fill with boiling water.

HINT: It is easier to place the tin in your oven and bring the kettle to the tin to fill it, rather than to try to carry a tin full of hot water.

Bake in the oven for 50 minutes. Take it out and leave for about 15 minutes to cool down slowly. Take off the lid and place foil on top and then a 900 g/2 lb weight. Place in the refrigerator for 12 hours.

To serve
Turn out of the terrine and serve on a platter with some parsley around to decorate, or cut and serve directly from the terrine. You can put the lid back on and leave in the refrigerator for about 2 weeks. Once it has been cut into, eat within 4–5 days.

SAUCISSON EN BRIOCHE
Brioche with Sausage

Brioche is a sweet yeast dough often used in French cuisine. We have all experienced those marvellous breakfast rolls. Here is another way of enjoying a brioche. The dough is made the night before and then set to rise and baked the next morning. In this recipe the dough surrounds a French sausage and is served with a light mustard sauce. It may also be used as a base for a tart, to encase pâtés, and as a base for different types of fillings. It is not difficult to make, and it can be made ahead and frozen.

Cooking time: 25 minutes To serve: 8–10

INGREDIENTS	METRIC	IMPERIAL	AMERICAN
Fresh yeast	15 g	½ oz	1 tbsp
Sugar to activate yeast	2.5 g	½ tsp	½ tsp
Water, tepid	25 ml	2 tbsp	2 tbsp
Plain flour	250 g	9 oz	1 cup + 1 tbsp
Salt	2.5 g	½ tsp	½ tsp
Sugar	20 g	¾ oz	1½ tbsp
Eggs	4	4	4
Unsalted butter	125 g	4½ oz	½ cup + 1 tbsp

French cooked sausage in one piece, cut, if necessary, to fit the length of a loaf tin (any type of cooked sausage will do). It should be about 6.5 cm/2½ in in diameter, and should have a texture that can easily be sliced with the brioche.

FOR EGG WASH:			
Egg	1	1	1
Water	15 ml	1 tbsp	1 tbsp

To activate the yeast
Add 30 ml/2 tablespoons of tepid water (it should not feel hot or cold to the touch) and 2.5 g/½ teaspoon of sugar to the yeast. After about

Saucisson en Brioche

5 minutes, it should start to foam and form a slight head. (If it doesn't, do not use it; get some fresh yeast and start again.)

To make the dough
Place the flour, salt and sugar in large mixing bowl. Make a well in the centre of the flour and mix the eggs and yeast in it. Slowly beat all the flour into the hole. Beat with a wooden spoon in an upward motion to aerate the dough for 5 minutes. This will make the dough uniform.

Cream the butter so that it is soft. Beat the butter into the dough and continue to beat for 10 minutes. The dough should be elastic and satiny. Cover with a tea cloth and then a plate and put in the refrigerator for 2 hours. Take out and beat for another 5 minutes. Put in the refrigerator, covered in the same way, overnight. The next day take out the dough and beat for 10 minutes. It must become supple to rise properly.

To set to rise
Grease a loaf tin and put a layer of dough in the bottom. Lay the sausage in the centre lengthwise. Put the rest of the dough on top of the sausage, making sure the top and bottom layers are pressed together to encompass the sausage completely. Set to rise in a warm spot until it is double in size. This will take 2–3 hours.

To bake
Pre-heat the oven to 200°C/400°F/gas mark 6. Brush with an egg wash (egg mixed with a little water). This will give it a golden colour. Place in the oven and bake for 20–25 minutes. It is done when a knife inserted in the centre comes out clean. Take out of the pan and set on a cake rack to cool.

To serve
Slice the brioche and serve with mustard sauce.

HINTS ABOUT YEAST: Dry yeast will last about 6 months. To reconstitute it sprinkle 15 ml/1 tbsp in 50 ml/2 tbsp water sweetened with 15 ml/1 tsp sugar at a temperature of approximately 43°C/110°F.

SAUCE À LA MOUTARDE
Mustard Sauce

INGREDIENTS	METRIC	IMPERIAL	AMERICAN
FOR BÉCHAMEL SAUCE:			
Butter	20 g	¾ oz	1½ tbsp
Plain flour	20 g	¾ oz	1½ tbsp
Milk	300 ml	10 fl oz	1¼ cups
2 parsley stalks, 2 or 3 peppercorns, 1 bay leaf, 1 slice onion, 1 blade mace (this is the outer covering of the nutmeg) for infusion			
Dijon mustard	25 g	2 tbsp	2 tbsp
White wine vinegar	15 ml	1 tbsp	1 tbsp
Salt and freshly ground black pepper to taste			

To make the béchamel sauce

Melt the butter in a saucepan. Remove from the heat, add the flour and stir. This should give you a slack or loose roux. If the roux is thick add a little more butter.

Meanwhile warm the milk with the infusion to tepid. (This means it feels neither hot nor cold to the touch.) Strain the milk into the roux all at once and stir over the heat until bubbles appear. This will cook the flour. The sauce will be thick and shiny. Add salt and pepper to taste.

To finish the sauce

Add the mustard and wine vinegar to the warm sauce. Taste and add more mustard if needed. Add salt and pepper. Serve with the brioche. The sauce may be made in advance and covered with a buttered piece of greaseproof paper to prevent a skin from forming. If it becomes too thick on standing, add a little warm milk.

PÂTE BRISÉE
Shortcrust Pastry

This is a basic shortcrust pastry recipe. It can be varied in many ways. The amounts called for will fill a 20 cm/8 in flan ring or 23 cm/9 in pie dish. It will also cover 6 small tart tins.

Some hints about making pastry

The secret of success is to have everything cold. The fat should be just out of the refrigerator and the water ice cold. When rubbing in the fat, try to work with the tips of your fingers. These will be cooler than the palm of your hands. You must try to keep the fat from melting into the flour. It is easy to cut the fat into the flour in a food processor. I prefer, however, to work by hand thereafter.

If your flour starts turning a yellow colour this means the fat is melting. Place the bowl immediately in the refrigerator or freezer to cool.

Try not to overwork the pastry once the water has been added, this will toughen it.

Use plain flour. Self-raising flour will give a spongy result. Mixing a white fat with a yellow fat will give you a flakier crust.

INGREDIENTS	METRIC	IMPERIAL	AMERICAN
Plain flour	225 g	8 oz	1 cup
Butter or margarine	75 g	3 oz	⅓ cup
White vegetable fat or lard	25 g	1 oz	2 tbsp
Iced water	60 ml	4 tbsp	about ¼ cup
Salt	5 g	1 tsp	1 tsp

Sift the flour and salt together into a bowl. Cut the fat into the flour. This may be done with a pastry blender or by using 2 knives. Rub in the fat with your fingertips so there are no large lumps. The mixture should resemble breadcrumbs. Make a well in the centre of the mixture and add a little water. Mix it in with a palette knife or other knife and add more water to the drier areas as needed.

HINT: You may need more or less water than called for. The amount of moisture in the flour determines how much more you need to add. In the winter, flour seems to be dry, while in humid or hot weather it can be heavy with moisture.

When the mixture starts to come together in a ball, knead it lightly with your hands. Many people feel that pastry needs some of the acid from your hands to be really good. Don't overknead. Wrap in a polythene bag and place in the refrigerator to rest. The gluten needs time to relax before baking.

TARTES NORMANDES
Normandy Tartlets

These tartlets have a most interesting texture and flavour. They include all the good things that Normandy has to offer including cream, cheese and Calvados (or apple brandy). The tartlets are made in layers which is both pretty and allows you to taste the separate flavours which produce a savoury blend. They make a wonderful luncheon dish.

Cooking time: about 30 minutes To serve: 6

INGREDIENTS	METRIC	IMPERIAL	AMERICAN
Pâte brisée (shortcrust pastry)	225 g	8 oz	1 cup
Ham, chopped	75 g	3 oz	1/3 cup
Calvados (or other apple brandy)	25 ml	2 tbsp	2 tbsp
FOR THE THICK BÉCHAMEL SAUCE:			
Butter	50 g	2 oz	1/4 cup
Plain flour	40 g	1½ oz	2½ tbsp
Milk	225 ml	8 oz	1 cup
Salt and white pepper to taste			
TO FINISH			
Tomato purée (paste)	15 ml	1 tbsp	1 tbsp
Cheddar or Emmental cheese, grated	50 g	2 oz	1/4 cup
Crème fraîche	80 ml	6 tbsp	6 tbsp

6 small tartlet tins about 11.6 cm/4½ in diameter if serving as luncheon or supper dish, about 9 cm/3½ in if serving for a first course.

To prepare and bake the tarts
Line the tins with the pastry and bake blind. Place tissue paper or greaseproof paper over the pastry and fill the tin with dried beans, rice, stale breadcrumbs or anything that will serve to weigh down the pastry. Bake at 170°C/350°C gas mark 4 for 15 minutes. Take out and remove the beans etc. and paper. Place back in the oven for 5 minutes to complete the baking. The tarts should be golden in colour and cooked through. Take out to cool, and remove from the tins to a baking tray.

To prepare the filling
Make the béchamel sauce: Melt the butter in a saucepan. Remove from the heat, add the flour and stir. This should give you a slack or loose roux. If the roux is thick add a little more butter. Meanwhile warm the milk to tepid. (This means when you touch it, it feels neither too hot nor too cold.) Pour the milk into the roux all at once and stir over the heat until bubbles appear. This will cook the flour. The sauce will be thick and shiny. Add salt and pepper to taste.

Add the chopped ham and 15 ml/1 tablespoon of Calvados to the sauce and mix well.

To finish
Add the tomato purée and the remainder of the Calvados to the crème fraîche.

To serve
Fill the cooked tarts three-quarters full with the béchamel sauce. Spoon on the crème fraiche and sprinkle the grated cheese on top. Place under a hot grill to warm through and melt the cheese. Serve immediately.

HINT: If you wish to prepare this in advance, get everything ready but do not fill the pastry. Place a piece of buttered greaseproof paper over the sauce to prevent a skin from forming. Just before serving, warm the béchamel through and then complete filling the tarts.

TARTE À L'OIGNON
Onion Tart

This celebrated French dish is in the tradition of fine French cuisine. When the flavour of your dish depends on a key ingredient, it should be of good quality. The secret of success here is similar to that of onion soup; and that is cooking the onions very slowly to bring out their sweetness and flavour. The method of sweating onions that has been used throughout this book is employed here to prepare this dish with a minimum of effort.

Cooking time: 35 minutes To serve: 6–8

INGREDIENTS	METRIC	IMPERIAL	AMERICAN
One 20 cm or 23 cm/8 in or 9 in tart tin lined with shortcrust pastry (see pâte brisée recipe on page 32)			
FOR THE BÉCHAMEL SAUCE:			
Butter	20 g	¾ oz	1½ tbsp
Plain flour	20 g	¾ oz	1½ tbsp
Milk	300 ml	10 fl oz	1¼ cups
2 parsley stalks, 2 or 3 peppercorns, 1 bay leaf, 1 slice onion, 1 blade mace (this is the outer covering of the nutmeg) for infusion			
Salt and freshly ground black pepper to taste			
Onions, finely sliced	680 g	1½ lb	1½ lb
Butter	50 g	2 oz	4 tbsp
Water	50 ml	2 fl oz	½ cup

Pre-heat the oven to 220°C/425°F/gas mark 7.

To bake the pastry blind
Place a piece of greaseproof paper or tissue paper in the lined tin. Fill the tin with dried beans, rice, stale breadcrumbs or anything to weight down the tart. Bake for 15 minutes. Take out and remove the beans and paper. Set aside.

To make the béchamel sauce
Melt the butter in a saucepan. Remove from the heat, add the flour and stir. This should give you a slack or loose roux. If the roux is thick add a little more butter. Meanwhile warm the milk with the infusion ingredients until it is tepid. (This means when you touch it, it feels neither hot or cold to the touch.) Strain the milk into the roux all at once and stir over the heat until bubbles appear. This will cook the flour. The sauce will be thick and shiny. Add salt and pepper to taste.

To sauté the onions
Melt the butter in large frying pan and add the onions. Sauté for 2 minutes. Add the water and cover with a piece of greaseproof paper and a lid. Let sweat on a low heat until the onions are transparent. This could take 10–15 minutes. Remove the lid and paper and continue to sauté until the onions take on a golden colour; about another 5 minutes.

To bake
Fill the tart one third full with the béchamel sauce. Spread the onions evenly over the tart. Place in the oven and cook for 20 minutes.

To serve
Serve the tart directly from the oven. If you wish, prepare everything in advance but do not fill the tart as it will become soggy. Fill the tart and bake just before serving. This recipe also works very well for individual tartlets.

Quiche Fantaisie (top), (p 36), Tarte à l'Oignon (bottom)

QUICHE FANTAISIE
Fantasy Quiche

This is a delightful, crustless quiche with a pleasing combination of flavours. It easily becomes a favourite. Use it for supper, lunch, at a buffet or for a first course. Since it doesn't have a crust, it can be prepared a day before.

Cooking time: about 50 minutes To serve: 6–8

INGREDIENTS	METRIC	IMPERIAL	AMERICAN
Butter	25 g	1 oz	2 tbsp
Breadcrumbs, toasted	100 g	4 oz	½ cup
FOR THE CREAMY MUSHROOM FILLING:			
Butter	25 g	1 oz	2 tbsp
Button mushrooms, sliced	450 g	1 lb	1 lb
Milk	120 ml	4 fl oz	½ cup
FOR THE CHEESE FILLING:			
Cottage cheese	100 g	4 oz	½ cup
Crème fraîche	140 ml	5 fl oz	½ cup + 1 tbsp
Eggs	2	2	2
Chopped parsley and tarragon mixed. (If using dried herbs, use half the amount). Fresh thyme and oregano may be substituted	15 g	1 tbsp	1 tbsp
Nutmeg	5 g	1 tsp	1 tsp
Salt and freshly ground black pepper to taste			
FOR THE OMELETTE:			
Butter	25 g	1 oz	2 tbsp
Egg	1	1	1
Salt and freshly ground black pepper to taste			
TO FINISH:			
Ham, diced	140 g	5 oz	5 oz

25 cm/10 in quiche dish (one that can be brought to the table is useful) prepared with: 25 g/1 oz/2 tbsp butter and 225 g/8 oz/1 cup breadcrumbs

Pre-heat the oven to 180°C/350°F gas mark 4.

To prepare the quiche dish
Generously butter the dish and press the breadcrumbs into the butter, making sure the bottom and sides are covered. Refrigerate to set.

To prepare the mushroom filling
Heat the butter in a frying pan and sauté the mushrooms for about 3 minutes. Reduce the heat, cover with the milk and simmer until almost all the liquid has evaporated. This will take about 15–20 minutes.

To make the cheese filling
Combine the cottage cheese and half of the créme fraiche and mix well with an electric beater or in a food processor. Mix in the eggs, herbs and seasonings and blend well.

To make the omelette:
Melt the butter in an omelette pan or small frying pan. Beat the egg and season. Add the egg and tilt the pan so that the egg covers the bottom. When it is set, take the quiche pan out of the refrigerator and gently slide the omelette into the breadcrumb base.

To assemble and bake
Spread the creamy mushroom filling over the omelette. Pour the cheese filling over the mushrooms and sprinkle with the ham. Bake for 35–40 minutes until set. The quiche may be made a day ahead to this point. Cover and refrigerate.

To finish and serve
Twenty minutes before serving spread the remaining crème fraiche over the top and bake at 180°C/350°F gas mark 4 until the cream is set. This will take about 10–15 minutes. Serve immediately.

CRÊPES
Crêpes

Crêpes are loved by everyone. Perhaps this is because of our memories of *Mardi Gras* or Shrove Tuesday. Crêpes are really very simple to make and are so useful in many recipes. Since they can be made ahead, they make an easy first course or luncheon dish. Store them in a plastic bag in the refrigerator or in your freezer. In many cases, depending upon the type of filling used, they can also be frozen, with their fillings, on a serving platter and then easily defrosted, warmed and served.

Cooking time: 15 minutes To serve: 6

INGREDIENTS	METRIC	IMPERIAL	AMERICAN
Plain flour	100 g	4 oz	½ cup
Salt	5 g	1 tsp	1 tsp
Egg	1	1	1
Milk	300 ml	10 oz	1¼ cup
Melted butter or salad oil	15 ml	1 tbsp	1 tbsp
Butter for cooking	75 g	3 oz	⅓ cup

Sift the flour and salt into a large bowl. Make a well in the flour and add the beaten egg. Add the milk slowly, pouring it into the well stirring constantly. Slowly incorporate the flour as you stir. When all the flour has been incorporated, stir in the fat. Mix until smooth. Let stand for 30 minutes. It should have the consistency of thick cream. This amount should make 15 crêpes.

To cook

Generously brush melted butter over the surface of your crêpe pan and heat the pan until the fat is smoking. Pour just enough batter into the pan to make a thin coating.

HINT: You will get to know just how much batter you need to cover the bottom of the pan. I usually use half a ladle full. The first crêpe is usually not your best. It takes at least one crêpe to get your pan to the right temperature.

If you have poured too much batter into the pan, pour some off. You want your crêpes to be as thin as possible. When you can slip a palate knife under the crêpe it is ready for turning. Loosen the crêpe by slipping the knife all the way under the crêpe and turning it with the knife. Cook for a few seconds on the other side and turn out onto a cake rack covered with a clean tea towel. Continue making the crêpes. Make sure the fat is smoking each time before you pour more batter in. Each crêpe should be turned out onto the last crêpe. You do not need to put paper between them. While each crêpe is cooking, cover the warm ones with part of the tea towel.

HINT: Using a cake rack keeps air circulating under the crêpes and in this way they do not steam while sitting.

CRÊPES AU JAMBON FLAMBÉS AU COGNAC
Ham Crêpes, Flambéd in Cognac

This is a light crêpe filling which is enhanced by the mixture of apricot brandy and cognac flambéd together. The crêpes can be filled and rolled in advance and warmed in an oven and flambéd just before serving.

Cooking time: 10 minutes To serve: 6

12, 15 cm/6 in crêpes made from the basic crêpe recipe (Two crêpes per person is sufficient for a first course. However if you wish to serve more, alter the quantities accordingly.)

INGREDIENTS	METRIC	IMPERIAL	AMERICAN
Butter	25 g	1 oz	2 tbsp
Good quality ham, coarsely chopped	450 g	1 lb	1 lb
Crème fraîche or double (heavy) cream	225 ml	8 oz	1 cup
Cognac	120 ml	4 oz	½ cup
Apricot brandy	120 ml	4 oz	½ cup

Melt the butter in a frying pan and sauté the ham for 1–2 minutes. Add the *crème fraîche* to the pan and simmer for 2 more minutes.

To fill the crêpes

Place the crêpes on a counter in front of you and put a large spoonful of the mixture near the edge of each crêpe. Roll the crêpes up and place them side by side on an ovenproof serving platter.

The recipe can be made ahead to this point. Brush the crêpes with melted butter to keep them from drying out.

To finish

Place in a warm oven 190°C/375°F/gas mark 5 for 5 minutes to warm through. If the crêpes have been made several hours in advance they will need a few minutes longer in the oven. Warm the cognac and apricot brandy in a saucepan. To flambé, tip the pan slightly so that the gas flame will ignite the liquid. If using an electric hob, throw a lighted match into the warm liquid. (Remember to remove the match before serving.)

To serve

Quickly pour the flaming liquid over the crêpes and serve immediately. The liquid will continue to burn if you keep stirring it with a spoon.

HINT: You may find it easier to bring the crêpes to the table on their serving platter and then bring in the sauce separately. I have a pretty little copper saucepan that I bring to the table in this way. I light it in the kitchen and continue to stir it with a spoon while I bring it to the table and pour the liquid over the crêpes. The flame is not very hot and you do not need to worry about burning your hands.

Crêpes: (clockwise) Gâteau de Crêpes (p 40), Crêpes au Saumon Fumé (p 40), Crêpes au Jambon

CRÊPES AU SAUMON FUMÉ

Smoked Salmon Crêpes

This is an easy and very elegant first course. The crêpes can be made ahead and kept in the refrigerator or frozen. The dish can easily be assembled a few hours before your guests arrive.

Cooking time: 5 minutes To serve: 6

INGREDIENTS	METRIC	IMPERIAL	AMERICAN
12, 15 cm/6 in crêpes made from the basic crêpe recipe with 15 g/1 tbsp of chopped dill added to the batter. (Two crêpes per person is sufficient for a first course, however; if you wish to serve more, alter the quantities accordingly.)			
Fresh dill, chopped	45 g	3 tbsp	½ cup
Smoked salmon, thinly sliced	100 g	4 oz	4 oz
Soured cream	85 ml	6 tbsp	6 tbsp
TO GARNISH:			
Fresh sprigs of dill, parsley or watercress.			

Prepare the crêpe batter. Cook in the normal way using a 15 cm/6 in crêpe pan. When ready to serve, place the crêpes in a warm oven to warm through. Mix the rest of the dill into the soured cream. Open the crêpes on a counter and place 7 ml/½ tablespoonful of soured cream in the centre of each one. Place a small slice of salmon on the cream, laying it so that a little of the salmon sticks out from the crêpe. Fold the crêpe in half and then in half again to make a triangle.

To serve

Place the crêpes in a row on a serving platter and decorate with sprigs of fresh herbs.

GÂTEAU DE CRÊPES

Crêpes Layered with Savoury Fillings

Here is another way of serving crêpes. The crêpes are layered flat one on top of the other with colourful fillings sandwiched in between. When sliced like a cake, the varied layers are very attractive. This is a good dish for using up various leftovers from your refrigerator. Tired vegetables can be made into purées; pieces of meat mixed with some béchamel sauce; stray bits of cheese grated and melted.

Cooking time: about 30 minutes To serve: 6–8

INGREDIENTS	METRIC	IMPERIAL	AMERICAN
FOR A TOMATO SAUCE FILLING:			
Onion, chopped	1 med	1 med	1 med
Butter	25 g	1 oz	2 tbsp
Garlic, crushed	1 clove	1 clove	1 clove
Ripe tomatoes, quartered	450 g	1 lb	1 lb
Bouquet garni (1 bay leaf, 2 branches thyme, several parsley stalks, all tied together)			
Salt and freshly ground black pepper to taste			
Large pinch of sugar			
FOR A CHEESE FILLING:			
Curd cheese (Philadelphia style cream cheese or fromage blanc may be substituted.)	50 g	2 oz	¼ cup
Double cream	40 ml	3 tbsp	3 tbsp
Blue cheese, crumbled or mashed	25 g	1 oz	2 tbsp
Fresh parsley, chopped	25 g	2 tbsp	2 tbsp
Freshly ground black pepper			
FOR A SPINACH FILLING:			
Fresh spinach, washed and stemmed	450 g	1 lb	1 lb

(Frozen spinach may be used. Be sure to cook it until it's dry.)

Onion, chopped	1 small	1 small	1 small
Butter or margarine	25 g	1 oz	2 tbsp
Double cream	60 ml	4 tbsp	4 tbsp
Freshly grated nutmeg	5 g	1 tsp	1 tsp
Salt and freshly ground black pepper to taste			

TO GARNISH:

Cheddar or Emmental cheese, grated	50 g	2 oz	¼ cup
A little of the above tomato sauce			

Make 12, 20 cm/8 in crêpes using the basic recipe.

To make tomato sauce

Sweat the onions in the butter until transparent. Add the garlic, then the tomatoes and bouquet garni. Cover and simmer for about 10 minutes. The tomatoes will cook to a sauce. If your tomatoes aren't ripe it may take longer. Remove the bouquet garni. Purée the mixture in a food processor, put through a food mill or simply sieve. If it is still quite liquid, place back on the heat to reduce. It should have the consistency of thick tomato sauce. Add salt and pepper to taste. Add the sugar. Tomatoes contain a lot of acid and need a little sweetener. Taste and correct seasoning as necessary. This sauce may be made in advance and stored in the refrigerator or freezer.

To make the cheese filling

In a food processor or with an electric beater, blend the curd cheese with the cream and add the blue cheese and parsley. Add the pepper. The cheese contains a lot of salt so only add salt after tasting if you think it necessary. Set aside. If you make the dish and keep it in the refrigerator, allow it to warm to room temperature before using.

To make the spinach filling

To blanch the spinach leaves, place in boiling water. When the water comes back to the boil, drain and refresh in cold water. Take the spinach and squeeze it out between two plates to remove any excess liquid. Chop with a knife or in a food processor. Sweat the onions as for tomato sauce above. Add the spinach and cook to dry out the spinach. Add the cream and seasonings. Taste and add more nutmeg, salt or pepper as needed.

To finish

Place 1 crêpe on an ovenproof serving plate and spread a little of the spinach mixture on it, as if it were a sandwich. Place another crêpe on top and spread with the cheese mixture. Place a third crêpe on top and spread with some tomato sauce. Spread the sauces evenly on the crêpes, but don't overfill them or the sauces will ooze out. Continue layering the crêpes in this manner. Leave the top crêpe free and pour a little of the tomato sauce over the top. Sprinkle the grated cheese on top and place in 190°C/375°F/gas mark 5 oven for 15 minutes to warm through and melt the cheese topping.

HINT: The crêpes may be filled several hours before your guests arrive. Add the sauce on top and cheese just before placing in the oven.

To serve

Slice in wedges to serve. The crêpes may be re-warmed in a microwave, or gently in an oven.

ROULADE AUX ÉPINARDS
Spinach Soufflé Roll

The delicate texture and blend of flavours make this a special first course. It is a spinach soufflé, rolled and filled with a mushroom sauce. It makes a lovely luncheon dish served with tomato sauce, or it can be served as a vegetable to dress up your main course.

Cooking time: 20 minutes To serve: 6–8

INGREDIENTS	METRIC	IMPERIAL	AMERICAN
Fresh spinach, washed, stems removed (10 oz frozen spinach, may be used)	900 g	2 lbs	2 lbs
Butter	25 g	1 oz	2 tbsp
Freshly grated Parmesan	15 g	½ oz	2 tbsp
Eggs, separated	4	4	4
FOR THE MUSHROOM FILLING:			
Mushrooms	175 g	6 oz	1½ cups
Butter	25 g	1 oz	2 tbsp
Plain flour	15 g	1 tbsp	1 tbsp
Single cream	70 ml	2½ fl oz	⅓ cup
Freshly ground nutmeg	2.5 g	½ tsp	½ tsp
Salt and freshly ground black pepper to taste			
Swiss roll tin or baking sheet			
Foil			
Butter to grease foil	25 g	1 oz	2 tbs

Pre-heat oven to 180°C/350°F/gas mark 4.

To prepare Swiss roll tin or baking sheet
Cut a piece of foil to fit the bottom of the tin and generously grease the paper. Set aside.

To make the spinach soufflé
If using fresh spinach place in a large pan with about 50ml/2 fl oz of water and cook until tender. Drain thoroughly. Place between two plates

Tipping the roulade out onto a cloth

and squeeze out as much water as possible. Chop either on a board or in a food processor or run through a food mill. Place back in the saucepan with the butter and cook until completely dry. If the spinach is not dry, the soufflé will be soggy from the moisture. If using frozen spinach cook according to the packet instructions and dry out with butter as above. Take off the heat and add the Parmesan cheese and egg yolks. Mix well.

Whisk the egg whites to a stiff peak. Fold a large spoonful of whites into the spinach mixture. This will lighten the mixture and make it easier to fold into the whites. Carefully fold the spinach mixture into the whites. Try not to overfold. Spread evenly onto the prepared Swiss

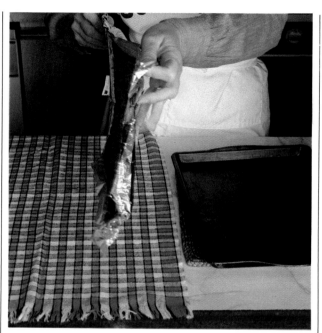

Rolling up the roulade

Roulade aux Épinards

roll tin and place in the oven. Bake for 7–10 minutes. It should be firm to the touch when done. If your finger leaves a print on the surface, then it needs a few minutes longer. When the soufflé is done, take it out and turn out onto a clean tea towel. The best way to do this is to take hold of the foil at two corners and flip the soufflé over onto the tea towel.

To make the filling
Wash the mushrooms.

> *HINT: The best way to clean mushrooms is to wipe them with a damp piece of kitchen paper. If you soak them under running water, they will become water logged and soggy.*

Chop the mushrooms and sauté in butter for 2 minutes. Draw to the side of the pan and add the flour. Mix thoroughly and add the cream. Place on the heat and simmer to cook the flour. Add the nutmeg, salt and pepper to taste. Take off the heat and keep warm by covering.

To finish
Spread the filling onto the soufflé and roll up. Take hold of the tea towel and gently start to roll using the towel to lift and start the spiral. Roll onto a serving plate.

To serve
Slice the roll diagonally. Serve immediately.

Although this is at its best when served immediately, it is still quite nice if made several hours in advance, rolled in foil and gently rewarmed in the oven prior to serving.

43

SOUFFLÉ AU FROMAGE
Cheese Soufflé

Soufflés are fun to serve. Everyone loves to see a light soufflé with a slightly golden crust whisked to the table. Contrary to what most people believe, soufflés are quite simple to make. If made properly the soufflé can be placed in a soufflé dish and kept waiting for an hour, before putting in the oven to cook. Since it takes about 25–30 minutes to cook, you can prepare the soufflé ready for the oven about 1½ hours before it is needed.

This is a basic recipe. Using the techniques described below, you can make other types of souffles by varying the ingredients.

HINT: If you prepare a soufflé in advance, place it in a draught-free area until ready to cook in the oven.

Cooking time: about 30 minutes To serve: 6

INGREDIENTS	METRIC	IMPERIAL	AMERICAN
Butter	50 g	2 oz	¼ cup
Plain flour	40 g	1½ oz	2½ tbsp
Milk	300 ml	10 oz	1¼ cup
Infusion for milk: 1 bay leaf, 1 slice of onion, 4 peppercorns, 1 slice of carrot, a blade of mace (This is the outer covering of nutmeg and comes in little strips or blades.)			
Eggs	4	4	4
Egg white	1	1	1
Pinch of cayenne			
Large pinch of nutmeg			
Cheddar cheese, grated	75 g	3 oz	⅓ cup
Parmesan cheese, grated	25 g	1 oz	2 tbsp
Salt and freshly ground black pepper to taste			
Soufflé dish (height approx. 10 cm/4 in diameter approximately 15 cm/6 in) prepared with: Butter	25 g	1 oz	2 tbsp
Greaseproof paper			
String			

Pre-heat the oven to 200°C/400°F gas mark 6.

To prepare the souffle case

Grease the inside of the soufflé dish with some butter. Sprinkle some of the grated cheese around the bottom and sides. It will stick to the sides and form a delicious crust when served. Make a collar by cutting a piece of greaseproof paper to encircle the dish. This allows the soufflé to rise out of the dish and protects it from draughts. Grease the paper so that the soufflé will be able to slide up easily as it rises. Tie the paper round the dish with some kitchen string.

HINT: Holding the paper in place while trying to tie some string tightly around can be tricky. An ordinary paper clip is a useful aid. Fit the paper around the dish and clip it together at the top edge. This will leave you two hands to tie the string.

To make béchamel sauce

Place all the ingredients for the infusion in the milk and bring to the boil. Let cool. Melt the butter in a saucepan. Remove from the heat, add the flour and stir. This should give you a slack or loose roux. If the roux is thick, add a little more butter. Meanwhile warm the milk until it is tepid (when you touch it, it should feel neither too hot nor too cold) and strain. Pour the milk into the roux all at once and stir over the heat until bubbles appear. This will cook the flour.

The sauce will be thick and shiny. Add salt and pepper to taste. Take off the heat.

HINT: If your sauce is too thick, (does not fall easily from a spoon) and heavy, then the soufflé will be the same. Add more warm milk to loosen the consistency if necessary. If your sauce is too liquid (has a watery consistency), then reduce it over gentle heat, stirring constantly until a thick creamy consistency is reached.

The béchamel can be made in advance. Place a piece of buttered paper or some melted butter over the top to prevent a skin from forming.

To make the soufflé

Separate the eggs. Beat the egg yolks into the sauce one at a time. Add the cayenne and nutmeg. Taste and add more seasoning if necessary. Beat all the egg whites to a stiff peak.

HINT: This is an important part of the soufflé process. The egg whites must reach a stiff peak without becoming dry. The best way to do this is in a copper bowl. Copper prevents the egg white from bleeding or becoming liquid and they will attain a third more volume. In addition, eggs whipped to a stiff peak will hold at least an hour in a copper bowl. However, using your electric beater in a glass bowl can achieve excellent results. Do not leave the whites in the bowl for even a minute. They will start to bleed and lose their bulk. Whip them up and use them immediately.

Mix one large spoonful of whites into the béchamel sauce. This will soften the sauce and make it easier to fold in the egg whites. Reserve one large spoonful of cheese to sprinkle on top. Stir the rest of the cheese into the sauce. Carefully fold the sauce into the egg whites trying not to fold too much. You want to leave as much air in the mixture as possible. Turn into the prepared soufflé dish. Sprinkle the reserved cheese on top. With a large spoon make a semi-circular cut in the top. This will allow some air to escape and form the traditional hat on top.

To bake

Place in the pre-heated oven on the middle shelf. Turn the oven down to 190°C/395°C/gas mark 5½. Leave for 20 minutes without opening the door. Check the soufflé. It should have risen and be golden on top. Leave 5 more minutes to set. The centre of the soufflé should be light and creamy. This forms the 'sauce' of the soufflé. Some people prefer the soufflé firm all the way through. In this case simply leave it in for 5 more minutes.

To serve

Cut the string and take off the paper. Put the dish on a serving platter and bring to the table. Break the top with a serving fork and spoon and serve in individual dishes, being careful to give each serving some of the sauce and some of the crust.

You may prefer to serve the souffle in individual ramekins. Grease the little ramekins and half fill each one with the mixture. You do not need to use a collar around each one. Bake for about 15–20 minutes. Serve immediately in the ramekins on serving dishes.

TIMBALES DE CAROTTES
Carrot Timbales

'Timbale' originally meant a small round metal receptacle intended to hold drinks. Today, it generally means anything cooked in a small round dish, such as a ramekin or dariole mould, and poached in a *bain-marie*. This carrot timbale is a delicate blend of flavours with fresh chervil as its secret ingredient. This fine herb with a slight aniseed taste is becoming better known in England. Many of the larger supermarkets have begun to stock it. If you cannot find it, use parsley and tarragon.

Cooking time: 25 minutes To serve: 6

INGREDIENTS	METRIC	IMPERIAL	AMERICAN
Carrots	680 g	1½ lbs	1½ lbs
Butter	25 g	3 tbsp	3 tbsp
Chicken stock	350 ml	12 oz	1½ cups
Castor sugar	5 g	1 tsp	1 tsp
Salt and freshly ground black pepper to taste			
FOR THE DUXELLES:			
Butter or margarine	25 g	1 oz	2 tbsp
Onion, chopped	1 small	1 small	1 small
Fresh mushrooms, finely chopped	175 g	6 oz	1½ cups
Eggs	3	3	3
Cheddar or Emmental cheese, grated	50 g	2 oz	¼ cup
Fresh chervil (or parsley and a few leaves of fresh tarragon) chopped			
TO GARNISH:			
Fresh spinach leaves	225 g	½ lb	2 cups
Fresh sprigs of chervil or parsley			
6 small ramekins or dariole moulds prepared with:			
Butter	25 g	1 oz	1 tbsp

Pre-heat the oven to 220°C/425°F/gas mark 7.

To prepare the moulds

Cut 6 circles of greaseproof paper to fit the bottom of the moulds. Brush some melted butter in the bottom of the mould. Place the paper in. Brush the paper and sides. Set aside.

To cook the carrots

Thinly slice the carrots. Melt the butter in a heavy-bottomed pan and add the carrots to sauté. Let them cook gently for 5 minutes. Add the chicken stock, sugar, salt and pepper. Cover and let simmer for another 5 minutes. Take the cover off and let all the liquid evaporate over a medium heat. Do not let them brown. This will take about 10–15 minutes. They should still be slightly wet.

To make the duxelles

Melt the butter in a small frying pan and add the chopped onion. Let the mixture sauté for several minutes. Add the chopped mushrooms. Sauté until all the liquid has evaporated.

To assemble and cook

Coarsely chop the carrots. Break up the eggs in a bowl and add the carrots, duxelles, cheese, chervil, and salt and pepper to taste. Mix together gently. Divide the mixture among the 6 moulds. Cover each mould with foil. Set in a roasting tin three-quarters filled with boiling water. Place in the oven for 20–25 minutes. They are done when firm to the touch and a knife inserted in the centre comes out clean.

To serve

Wash and dry the spinach leaves and herbs. Place one large, or several small spinach leaves on each plate to act as a base for the timbale. Slip a knife around the edge of the mould and turn out onto the leaves. Decorate with sprigs of chervil or parsley.

HINT: This dish is best served when it is just made, but it does re-warm very well. Leave the timbales in their moulds, replace in a bain-marie and place in the oven to warm through gently. Try not to dry them out. The timbales also re-warm very well in a microwave.

POIRE VINAIGRETTE
Pear Vinaigrette

A piquant sweet and sour dressing, and the use of fruit as a first course make this an intriguing dish. The secret is to choose pears that are beautifully ripe and sweet, and to make your sauce with just the right amount of tartness. Using lots of fresh mint adds the perfect touch.

Preparation time: 10 minutes To serve: 6

INGREDIENTS	METRIC	IMPERIAL	AMERICAN
Ripe pears	3	3	3
Lemon	1	1	1
FOR THE VINAIGRETTE:			
White wine vinegar	40 ml	3 tbsp	3 tbsp
Mustard	15 ml	1 tbsp	1 tbsp
Corn or sunflower oil	150 ml	5 fl oz	²/₃ cup
Salt and freshly ground black pepper to taste			
FOR THE GARNISH:			
Fresh mint, chopped	50 g	2 oz	¼ cup
Fresh parsley, chopped	50 g	2 oz	¼ cup
Lettuce leaves washed and dried, to decorate plates and sprigs of fresh mint to garnish (optional)			

To make the vinaigrette
Put the vinegar and mustard in a small bowl and whisk until smooth. Add the oil and whisk again. It should be smooth and creamy. Add salt and pepper to taste. Set aside. The dressing can be made well in advance, but is best if made on the day it is used.

To prepare the pears
Peel the pears over a bowl to catch any juices. Rub with a sliced lemon to prevent them from turning brown. Take the peelings and squeeze out any juices they may contain. Save the juice. Cut the pears in half lengthwise. Take out the core and stem. Pour the pear juice into the vinaigrette. Taste and correct seasoning if necessary. Mix in half of the herbs.

HINT: The dressing should be tart with a hint of fruit flavour. If your pears are very juicy then do not add all of the juice or add some lemon juice if needed.

To serve
Prepare individual serving plates by placing a layer of lettuce leaves on each. Place a pear half round side up on the leaves and spoon a generous helping of dressing over it. Sprinkle the reserved herbs on top and decorate with the sprigs of fresh mint. The dressing should be put on immediately, to keep the pears from turning brown. This dish can be made several hours before your guests arrive and placed on the table. For buffet serving, or if you prefer, the pears can be placed on one large serving platter instead of individual plates.

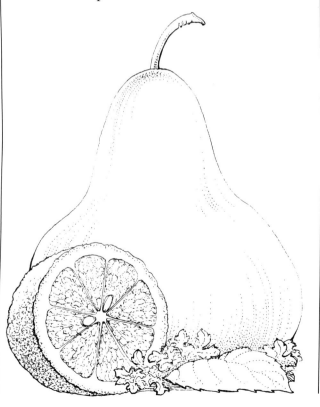

ASPÈRGES
Asparagus

Fresh asparagus is spring-time treat. Asparagus can be green, white or purple. It is really a matter of personal taste as to which one you choose. In general, the best white asparagus comes from Belgium. It is not allowed to see the sun and therefore does not turn green. The purple asparagus originated in Genoa, while the green asparagus came from France. Today, it is grown all over the world. I personally like the green asparagus because, as the French say, 'it has the taste of the sun in it'. The very small thin asparagus are sweet and delicious and are used as asparagus tips. The only place I have been able to find these is in my father-in-law's garden. If you are lucky enough to have them, do not peel them, but simply boil for 10–15 minutes. When buying asparagus, look for crisp ones with compact tips. They should be moist at the butt end. Buy them separately if possible so that you can examine each one.

Cooking time: 20 minutes To serve: 6

INGREDIENTS	METRIC	IMPERIAL	AMERICAN
Asparagus	680–900 g	1½-2 lb	1½-2 lb
You should serve about 5–6 thick ones per person.			
Salt and freshly ground black pepper to taste			

Carefully peel the stalk starting from the butt end. Stop just before the tip. Cut off the hard part of the butt end. Tie the stalks together in a bundle. If you have an asparagus steamer, place them in the basket and steam for 15–20 minutes. A steamer is not necessary to achieve perfect results. They can be cooked by placing them standing up in a pot of salted boiling water. The water should come 5 cm/2 in up the stalk and the pot should be big enough to allow the asparagus to lie down. Lay 2 wooden spoons criss-cross in the pot to support them. Boil for 5 minutes. Pour another 2.5 cm/1 in of boiling water into the pot. Cook for a further 5 minutes. Lay the asparagus down and cook for 10 more minutes. They should be tender, but not limp and droopy. Carefully lift out of the water and place on a rack to drain.

HINT: The purpose of first cooking the stems is to allow these to cook through without overcooking the tips.

To serve
The asparagus can be left at room temperature and served cold with a vinaigrette sauce (page 75), or it can be served warm with melted butter.

HINT: The asparagus may be cooked ahead and kept at room temperature. Just before serving, place them in boiling water for 1–2 minutes simply to warm through.

LES POTAGES
SOUPS

What is more inviting on a cold dark winter's evening than a cheery table laden with bowls of hot colourful soup and perhaps some fresh bread to go with it? Or what could be more appealing on a hot summer's night than a chilled bowl of light, refreshing soup served with some mint or cucumber?

Throughout history soups have been the mainstay of our diet. Today they are very often the forgotten or lowly member of the food table.

Once a few simple techniques for making soups are understood, one can happily create many interesting, tasty and attractive dishes to grace the table and fill the stomachs of a hungry group.

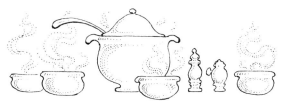

General Hints for Soup Making

For vegetable soups, the general rule of proportions is 400 g/14 oz of vegetables to 1 litre/32 oz of liquid. For a thick texture without the use of thickeners, a good jellied stock is preferable. Stock contains gelatine, a natural thickener, from whatever bones were used to produce it. There are certain vegetables, such as mushrooms, leeks and onions, that are also natural thickeners and when used in the correct proportions can result in a lovely thick soup 'au naturel'. We'll discuss these vegetables more later in the chapter. Thickening with stocks or vegetables has an added advantage: one can taste the full flavour of the ingredients without the taste being subdued by flour which tends to act as a flavour barrier. Whenever I do call for flour to thicken, I use it sparingly for this reason.

To finish soups with a lovely touch, garnish with fresh herbs or chopped nuts. I like to add a sprinkling to each bowl for colour or flavour. The warmth of the soup brings out the taste of the garnish. One of the herbs such as coriander, chives, mint, basil or parsley is usually available in the market. If you can't find them or can't get to the market, use freshly chopped nuts for an interesting flavour and texture complement to the soup.

Soups can be made in advance and frozen, which avoids last minute preparation when serving large groups.

The technique of sweating onions which is used throughout the book, is particularly important in soup making.

The recipes that follow illustrate these principles and, once learned and enjoyed, you will find you can create variations on your own.

POTAGE AU CRESSON
Watercress Soup

This will be a favourite for those interested in light, low calorie cuisine. Courgettes and leeks are used with the watercress and the soup becomes as thick as any cream soup without flour or other thickeners added. It can be served hot or cold. Its striking green colour and rich-looking texture will add elegance to your table.

Cooking time: 30 minutes   To serve: 6

INGREDIENTS	METRIC	IMPERIAL	AMERICAN
Butter	15 g	1 tbsp	1 tbsp
Leeks, whites only, cleaned and sliced	3	3	3
Courgettes, sliced	680 g	1½ lb	1½ lb
Chicken stock (or enough stock to cover the vegetables with an inch to spare).	1.7 l	3 pts	7½ cups
Salt and freshly ground black pepper to taste			
Watercress leaves	2 bunches	2 bunches	2 bunches
TO GARNISH:			
Chopped parsley, chives, or coriander leaves or a combination of fresh green herbs	75 g	6 tbsp	6 tbsp

Heat the butter in a large heavy-bottomed casserole and sweat the leeks until soft and transparent. Add the courgettes and sauté them for about 3 minutes, without browning. Cover with the stock and simmer until the courgettes are tender, about 20 min. Add a little salt and pepper. More will be added at the end.

Meanwhile wash the watercress carefully and take off the stems. The best way to do this is to place the bunches upside down in a bowl of water to be sure all the dirt floats out. Bring the soup to the boil and add the watercress. Add salt and pepper to taste. The amount depends on the freshness of the vegetables used. Taste for seasoning. Simmer for 1–2 minutes. Cool.

Purée the soup in a liquidiser. It should be very thick. If it is too thick, add more stock. Taste for seasoning.

To serve

Serve with some fresh chopped chives, fresh chopped mint or other fresh herb sprinkled on the soup, or serve cold with a spoonful of yogurt or crème fraîche in each bowl.

SOUPE AUX CHAMPIGNONS
Mushroom soup

One of the best known and loved of French soups, this is a wonderful choice for a dinner party.

Cooking time: 30 minutes   To serve: 6

INGREDIENTS	METRIC	IMPERIAL	AMERICAN
Onion, chopped	1 large	1 large	1 large
Butter	25 g	1 oz	2 tbsp
Mushrooms, washed and sliced	450 g	1 lb	1 lb
Flour	15 g	1 tbsp	1 tbsp
Chicken stock	720 ml	24 fl oz	1½ pt
Salt, pepper and freshly ground nutmeg to taste			

Sweat the onion in the butter until transparent. Add the mushrooms and sauté for 2 minutes.

Sprinkle the flour on top and stir until absorbed. Add the stock and bring to the boil. Lower the heat and simmer for 20 minutes. Add salt, pepper and nutmeg and taste for seasoning. This can be made one day ahead or earlier and frozen.

To serve

Serve hot from a tureen or in individual bowls.

Potage au Curry (1) (p 58), Potage aux Tomates et à l'Orange (middle) (p 55), Potage au Cresson (r)

POTAGE CRÈME DE LAITUE

Cream of Lettuce Soup

Every time I pass by the open markets and see the vendors throwing away the unwanted outside leaves of lettuce, I can't help but think what a waste and what a delicious soup they would make.

Here is a soup that has a delicate nutty flavour and can be made either from unwanted lettuce leaves, or by buying a couple of heads of lettuce.

This is an example of where the soup is thickened by the action of onions and the lactic acid in milk.

Cooking time: 30 minutes To serve: 6–8

INGREDIENTS	METRIC	IMPERIAL	AMERICAN
Lettuce, 2 large heads (round or batavia work well) or equivalent in lettuce leaves	2	2	2
Onion, finely chopped	1 med	1 med	1 med
Butter	25 g	1 oz	2 tbsp
Flour	20 g	¾ oz	¼ cup + 1 tbsp
Milk	850 ml	1½ pt	30 oz
Salt and freshly ground black pepper (to taste)			
TO GARNISH:			
Walnuts, finely chopped	100 g	4 oz	¼ lb
Fresh mint, chives or spring onions, finely chopped	75 g	6 tbsp	6 tbsp

Wash and dry the lettuce. Shred it finely. This can be done by slicing it in a food processor. Sweat the onions in the butter until transparent.

HINT: The onions should be carefully sweated or there will be difficulty with the milk curdling as the soup cooks.

When the onions are soft and clear, add the lettuce and stir gently. Draw the pan off the heat and stir in the flour. In a separate pan bring the milk to a boil and pour onto the lettuce and onions. Add salt and pepper. Simmer for 20 minutes. Do not boil. Pass through the fine sieve of a food mill or liquidise. Taste for seasoning and add more salt and pepper if necessary. It can be made one day ahead, or earlier, and frozen.

To serve

Sprinkle each serving with some chopped nuts and a fresh green herb such as chives, mint or the tops of spring onions, to add colour and flavour.

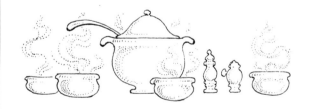

SOUPE À L'OSEILLE
Sorrel Soup

Sorrel (sometimes called sour grass) is a hardy herb that dates back to 300 BC. The French seem to be the only people to use it in quantity today. Its green leaves with their slightly lemony flavour are used for sauces, included in salads, added to vegetables such as spinach for extra flavour, or, as in this case, made into a superb soup.

As sorrel is the key ingredient and difficult to find here, you may need to ask your greengrocer to order it for you, or you can grow it in your own garden or on a window ledge. The leaves freeze well. Simply put them in a plastic bag in the freezer and use as needed.

Cooking time: 15 minutes To serve: 6

INGREDIENTS	METRIC	IMPERIAL	AMERICAN
Butter	25 g	1 oz	2 tbsp
Onion, finely chopped	1 med	1 med	1 med
Fresh or frozen sorrel, shredded	175 g	6 oz	1½ cups
Chicken stock	600 ml	1 pt	2½ cups
Salt and freshly ground black pepper to taste			
TO GARNISH:			
Crème fraîche	80 ml	6 tbsp	6 tbsp
Fresh parsley, chopped	75 g	6 tbsp	6 tbsp

Melt the butter in a saucepan and sweat the onion until transparent. Add the sorrel and then the stock. Cover and simmer for 5 minutes. Purée in a liquidiser or pass through the fine sieve of a food mill. Add salt and pepper to taste.

To serve
Heat to boiling and put one tablespoon of crème fraîche in each bowl. Pour the soup over the cream.

HINT: This soup is very good on its own without the crème fraîche. It is also good served with 3 egg yolks as a thickener. Just before serving, beat the yolks in a bowl and slowly pour the soup over them. Don't pour too quickly or the eggs will curdle.

POTAGE ST GERMAIN
Purée of Pea Soup

This is a St Germain with a difference; the addition of leeks and curry give it an added zest and character. It is best made a day in advance and is also quite good served at room temperature.

Cooking time: 30 minutes To serve: 6

INGREDIENTS	METRIC	IMPERIAL	AMERICAN
Leeks, whites only, finely sliced	3 large	3 large	3 large
Butter	50 g	2 oz	¼ cup
Lettuce, washed and shredded	1 head	1 head	1 head
Lemon juice	5 ml	1 tsp	1 tsp
Curry powder	15 g	1 tbsp	1 tbsp
Turmeric	5 g	1 tsp	1 tsp
Flour	25 g	2 tbsp	2 tbsp
Sugar	5 g	1 tsp	1 tsp
Fresh peas	680 g	1½ lb	1½ lb
or frozen peas	450 g	1 lb	1 lb
Chicken stock	600 ml	1 pt	20 oz
Salt and freshly ground black pepper to taste			
Single cream	120 ml	4 oz	½ cup
TO GARNISH:			
A few tiny raw peas, or freshly chopped chervil or mint.			

Sweat the leeks in the butter until transparent. Add the lettuce and lemon juice. When the lettuce has wilted, add the curry powder and turmeric and cook for a few minutes to release their flavour.

Stir in the flour. Add the sugar and a little salt and pepper and then the peas and stock. Simmer until the peas are very soft, about 15 minutes.

Liquidise or pass through the fine sieve of a food mill. If the mixture is too thick, add a little more chicken stock. Taste for seasoning and add more salt and pepper if necessary. Mix in the cream and serve.

To serve

Serve from a tureen with the raw baby peas or the mint or chervil floating on top; or serve individually with the same accompaniments.

POTAGE AUX ASPÈRGES
Asparagus Soup

(Illustrated on page 57)

One of the nicest things about wandering through the markets in spring is seeing the beautiful displays of fresh produce, especially asparagus. It not only makes a first-course treat but also a wonderful soup. I never waste anything if I can help it, and very often make this soup from the butt end of the asparagus.

Cooking time: 30 minutes To serve: 6

INGREDIENTS	METRIC	IMPERIAL	AMERICAN
Fresh asparagus (or an equal amount of butt ends)	680 g	1½ lb	1½ lb
Butter	75 g	3 oz	⅓ cup
Flour	40 g	3 tbs	3 tbsp
Chicken stock	350 ml	12 fl oz	12 fl oz
Water, taken from the water used to cook the asparagus	350 ml	12 fl oz	12 fl oz
Salt and freshly ground black pepper to taste			
TO GARNISH:			
Crème fraîche	80 ml	6 tbsp	6 tbsp
Fresh parsley, chopped	75 g	6 tbsp	6 tbsp

Peel the asparagus and plunge into enough boiling salted water to cover. Cook without a lid for 20 minutes or until tender. Take out and purée with a little of its cooking water either in a liquidiser, food processor or food mill.

Melt the butter in a saucepan and add the flour to form a roux. Stir for 1 minute to cook the flour. Add the stock and water and stir until smooth. Add the puréed asparagus. Stir until it boils, lower the heat and simmer for 5 minutes. Add salt and pepper to taste.

To serve

Put 1 tablespoon of crème fraîche in each bowl and pour the soup over it. Or serve in a soup tureen and add the cream to the tureen. Sprinkle some chopped parsley on top.

POTAGE AUX TOMATES ET À L'ORANGE
Tomato and Orange Soup

Whenever I mention this soup to my students, I receive looks of disbelief which are always quickly dispelled after the first taste. The unusual combination of tomatoes and oranges creates a mellow orange colour and a taste that teases the palate. It is delicious served hot with a spoonful of crème fraîche, or served cold with a spoonful of natural yogurt.

HINT: All the ingredients for this recipe can be sliced in a food processor which speeds things up considerably.

Cooking time: 1 hour 15 minutes To serve: 6–8

INGREDIENTS	METRIC	IMPERIAL	AMERICAN
Butter	25 g	1 oz	2 tbsp
Onion, thinly sliced	1 med	1 med	1 med
Carrot, thinly sliced	1 med	1 med	1 med
Lemon, thinly sliced (including skin)	1	1	1
Orange, thinly sliced (including skin)	1	1	1
Fresh tomatoes (drained canned tomatoes work well if fresh ones are out of season.)	900 g	2 lb	2 lb
Bouquet garni (1 bay leaf, a few parsley stalks, branch of thyme).			
Black peppercorns	5	5	5
Chicken stock	900 ml	32 fl oz	1 quart
Orange juice	225 ml	8 fl oz	1 cup
Butter	75 g	3 oz	1/3 cup
Flour	40 g	3 tbsp	3 tbsp
Salt and freshly ground black pepper to taste			
Sugar to taste, about	15 g	1 tbsp	1 tbsp
TO GARNISH:			
Crème fraîche or yogurt	100 g	4 fl oz	1/2 cup

HINT: If tomatoes are not in season, it is often a good idea to use canned tomatoes which have been processed at the peak of freshness. Fresh ones that have been flown in from great distances haven't as much flavour.

Place about 25 g/1 oz/2 tbsp of butter in a large saucepan and sweat the onions until they are transparent. Add the carrot and cook for 2–3 minutes. Add the lemon, orange, tomatoes, bouquet garni and peppercorns and pour in the stock and orange juice. Bring to the boil and let simmer uncovered for 1 hour. Sieve immediately. Do not purée.

HINT: Do not let the soup sit unsieved for any length of time. The pith from the orange and lemon will impart a bitter flavour.

Rinse the pan and add the 75 g/3 oz/1/3 cup of butter and then the flour. Cook for 1 minute. Add the sieved liquid and simmer for 10 minutes. Add salt, pepper and sugar to taste.

This soup can be made one day ahead or earlier and frozen.

To serve

Serve hot with a spoonful of crème fraîche in each bowl, or serve cold with a spoonful of natural yogurt in each serving.

VICHYSSOISE
Potato and Leek Soup

This very popular summer soup is, in fact, not truly French. Cold soups are not part of the French diet. The Americans took the basic hot leek and potato soup served throughout France, added more cream and some chives, and served it cold. They then exported it to France and it can be seen on some French menus today. I've included it, though, because it is easily prepared in advance and is a refreshing dish for warm evening entertaining.

Cooking time: 50 minutes To serve: 6

INGREDIENTS	METRIC	IMPERIAL	AMERICAN
Leeks, whites only, carefully washed and finely sliced	100 g	4 oz	1 cup
Onions, finely sliced	2 small	2 small	2 small
Butter	50 g	2 oz	¼ cup
Potatoes, peeled and sliced	450 g	1 lb	1 lb
Chicken stock	850 ml	1½ pt	3¾ cups
Salt and freshly ground white pepper to taste			
Double cream	225 ml	8 oz	1 cup
TO GARNISH:			
Fresh chives, chopped	75 g	6 tbsp	6 tbsp

HINT: It is best to cut chives with scissors rather than chop them.

All the vegetables can be sliced in a food processor. Sweat the leeks and onions in the butter in a large saucepan, until transparent. Add the potatoes and sauté for 5 more minutes. Add the stock, bring to a simmer and cook for 40 minutes. Add the salt and pepper and taste for seasoning. Liquidise or pass through the fine sieve of a food mill. Cool. The soup can be made ahead to this point. Stir in the cream before serving and taste again for seasoning.

Vichyssoise (above)

Potage aux Aspèrges (p 54) (left)

To serve
Serve at room temperature with chopped chives sprinkled on top. As this is a cold soup the bowls can be poured and placed on the table before the guests arrive.

HINT: Food that is served straight out of the refrigerator has less flavour. Try to bring it to room temperature before serving.

POTAGE AU CURRY
Curry Soup

I would be most surprised if any of your guests discovered that there was actually curry in this soup. It is an unusual blend of spices and a delicate balance of flavours. Served with the acidulated flavour of grated apple or a thin slice of lemon, it is sure to create a different taste sensation.

Cooking time: 30 minutes To serve: 6

INGREDIENTS	METRIC	IMPERIAL	AMERICAN
Desiccated coconut	15 g	1 tbsp	1 tbsp
Boiling water	425 ml	15 fl oz	2 cups
Butter	40 g	1½ oz	3 tbsp
Onion, finely chopped	1 small	1 small	1 small
Curry powder	5 g	1 tsp	1 tsp
Flour	15 g	½ oz	1 tbsp
Milk	425 ml	15 fl oz	2 cups
Chicken stock	425 ml	15 fl oz	2 cups
Double cream	25 ml	2 tbsp	2 tbsp
TO GARNISH:			
Apples grated and sprinkled with lemon juice (acidulated)	2	2	2

Make coconut milk by soaking the desiccated coconut in boiling water and leaving it to infuse for 15 minutes. Meanwhile, sweat the onions in the butter until transparent. Add the curry powder to the onions and cook for a few minutes. This will release the flavour in the powder.

HINT: Whenever working with powdered spices, it is a good idea to warm them either in a sauté pan, in the oven, on a plate over boiling liquid or even in a microwave. This will give the spices more flavour.

Stir in the flour and cook for 1 minute. Pour in the milk (not the coconut milk) and stock. Bring to the boil and simmer for 10 minutes. Strain the infusion of coconut and water and add the liquid to the soup. Pass the soup through a fine sieve or liquidise. Return to the pan, re-heat and add the cream.

To serve
The soup can be served with some grated apple that has been sprinkled with lemon juice to prevent the apples turning brown; or a thin slice of lemon can be floated in each bowl. Another interesting accompaniment is some plainly boiled rice that has been lightly coloured with paprika and is handed round separately.

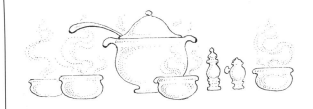

SOUPE À L'OIGNON
Onion Soup

Whenever I make this hearty French soup I am reminded of advice from my teacher in France. When I once mentioned that I was having dinner guests and was making onion soup, she immediately said, 'I hope you have told them what you will be serving. I always do.' She was afraid that I was going to insult my guests by serving this peasant dish at an elegant party. However, through the use of good quality ingredients, many 'peasant' dishes have been elevated to noble tables.

There are many versions of this classic French soup. One secret of this dish is the long slow cooking of the onions which brings out their sweet flavour. Properly sweating the onions plays an essential rôle. It is a good idea to make this soup a day in advance to allow all the flavours to blend together.

Cooking time: approximately 2 hours To serve: 6–8

INGREDIENTS	METRIC	IMPERIAL	AMERICAN
Butter	50 g	2 oz	¼ cup
Oil	15 ml	1 tbsp	1 tbsp
Onions, thinly sliced	900 g	2 lb	2 lb
Salt	5 g	1 tsp	1 tsp
Sugar	2.5 g	½ tsp	½ tsp
Flour	40 g	1½ oz	2 tbsp
Brown stock	1.7 l	3 pt	7½ cups
(If you are not using a good jellied stock, then use ¾ of the amount in chicken stock cubes and ¼ in beef stock cubes.)			
Dry white wine	150 ml	5 fl oz	¾ cup
Salt and freshly ground black pepper to taste			
TO GARNISH:			
Cognac (any type of brandy)	40 ml	3 tbsp	3 tbsp
Rounds of toasted French bread	6–8	6–8	6–8
Swiss cheese, grated	100 g	4 oz	½ cup
Parmesan cheese, freshly grated	100 g	4 oz	½ cup
Olive oil to pour over the bread rounds			

Place the butter and oil in a heavy-bottomed saucepan. Add the onions and sauté for 3–4 minutes. Add about 50 ml/2 fl oz of water and cover with greaseproof paper and then a lid. Cook very slowly for 15–20 minutes until the onions are transparent. Uncover, add the salt and sugar and cook for 30 minutes, stirring and watching carefully until the onions are a deep golden brown colour.

HINT: Adding the sugar will help to give a good colour and this will form the base of the rich flavour desired.

When all the liquid is evaporated and the onions look a rich golden brown, add the flour and cook for 1 minute. In a separate pan bring the stock and wine to the boil and pour onto the onions. Bring to the boil and lower the heat. Simmer with half a lid for about 50 minutes, skimming, if necessary, during this time. Add salt and pepper to taste.

To serve

Add the cognac to the soup and pour into a soup tureen, or place the bread in individual bowls and pour the soup over them. Mix the two cheeses together. Serve the cheese separately.

Another way of serving is to pour the soup into ovenproof bowls and float the bread on top. Sprinkle the grated cheese heavily over the top (about 50 g/2 oz per bowl) and then pour a little olive oil over it. Place in a hot oven for 20 minutes. Take out and place under a grill to brown.

SOUPE DE POISSON
Fish Soup from the Midi

Here is a famous French soup that has delighted visitors to the South of France for centuries. Its hearty aroma brings the sun of the Midi to a country-type dinner. Serve with aïoli (garlic mayonnaise) spread on rounds of French bread and floated in the soup.

In the South of France they make this with freshly caught fish that has not been washed, to keep all the sea-fresh flavour.

Cooking time: approximately 45 minutes To serve: 6–8

INGREDIENTS	METRIC	IMPERIAL	AMERICAN
Onions, thinly sliced (about 450 g/1 lb)	2 large	2 large	2 large
Olive oil	120 ml	4 fl oz	½ cup
Assorted fish steaks, (bass, whiting, porgy, sole)	1.8 kg	4 lb	4 lb
Tomatoes, sliced	4 large	4 large	4 large
Garlic, unpeeled, bruised (lightly tap them with the side of a knife to release their juices.)	10 cloves	10 cloves	10 cloves
Bouquet garni (6 sprigs of thyme, 1 bay leaf, several parsley stalks, a few slices of fresh fennel or some dried.)			
Water	2.4 l	4¾ pts	3 qts
Salt	5 g	1 tsp	1 tsp
Freshly ground black pepper to taste			
Whole saffron stems (tumeric may be used as a substitute. This will not give you the same flavour although the characteristic colour will be achieved.)	1.5 g	¼ tsp	¼ tsp

HINT: To make this a very inexpensive dish use 1.8 kg/4 lb of fish heads and bones. It gives all of the flavour and much more texture; or use a combination of fish and bones.

In a large pan sweat the onions in the olive oil until they are transparent. Add the fish and cook with the onions for about 10 minutes, stirring occasionally. Add the tomatoes, garlic and bouquet garni. Cook for a couple of minutes to combine the vegetables and fish. Add the water and salt and boil for about 20 minutes with half a lid. Purée through a food mill using a fine sieve. Place back in the saucepan, bring to the boil and reduce to 8 servings or 60 fl oz/3 pints. This should take about 10–15 minutes. Add the saffron and pepper. Taste for seasoning, adding more salt or pepper if necessary.

To serve:
Serve with aïoli sauce, French bread rounds and freshly grated Parmesan cheese.

Aïoli
Aïoli Sauce

INGREDIENTS	METRIC	IMPERIAL	AMERICAN
Egg yolk	1	1	1
Garlic, crushed	2 cloves	2 cloves	2 cloves
Dijon mustard (any mustard will do)	5 ml	1 tsp	1 tsp
Olive oil	150 ml	5 fl oz	⅔ cup
Salt and pepper to taste			

This may be made by hand or in a food processor or with an electric beater.

Beat the yolk, mustard, and garlic together until the yolk is slightly thickened. Add the oil drop by drop, beating constantly. When the mixture starts to resemble mayonnaise the oil may be added more quickly.

Soupe de Poisson avec Aïoli

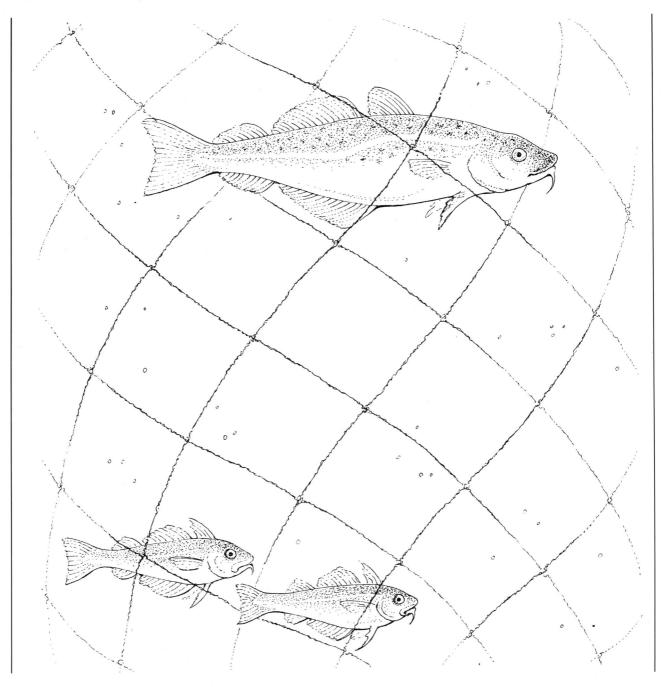

LES POISSONS
FISH

There are more than 20,000 kinds of fish in the world. This is as many types as amphibians, reptiles, birds and mammals added together. Thus, oceans, rivers and lakes hold an important source of food. Fish has been an important food throughout history. Louis XIV so loved fresh sea fish that he had it specially rushed from Boulogne and Dieppe to Versailles by relay teams. The horses on the fish carts were changed every few kilometres. Thus he was able to have his fish the day after it was caught. The populations of the Far East have always eaten more fish than those of the West. Today, however, our desire for fresh fish is growing, especially with the popularity of nouvelle cuisine *where fish plays an important role.*

The riches of the sea are there for the taking. The light texture and delicate flavour of fish can be enhanced by an accompanying sauce. This sauce, however, should be as light and delicate as the fish.

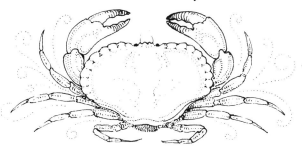

Hints on Buying and Cooking Fish

Fish comes either from fresh or salt water. The same species of fish that lives in salt water will be slightly different from its namesake found in fresh water. In fact, some of the most interesting and tasty fish comes from the northern Adriatic where the salt water mixes with fresh water that flows from the Alps. It will be very difficult for you to find the same fish in different areas. If you know that you want a certain type of fish but cannot find it, then your fishmonger can tell you what is the best and freshest substitute.

There are three basic rules to tell if a fish is fresh.

● The eyes should be shiny and clear and not sunken looking.

● The gills should be bright red.

● The flesh should be firm. When touched, the impression should not remain.

There is a fourth rule I usually follows. It should not smell 'fishy'. One of the best fish markets I have ever used, has absolutely no smell of fish when you enter. There is certainly no old fish there.

Fish should not be overcooked; it loses its flavour and texture. Remember, if the fish seems slightly underdone when you take it out of the pot, it will continue to cook in its own heat for a few more minutes.

POISSON EN PAPILLOTE
Steamed Fish Parcels

This is a wonderful method of steaming fish. All the natural juices are sealed into the packet which can be served directly at the table or can be opened in the kitchen and served onto the individual plates there. Everything can be made ready in advance and put in a hot oven just before serving. The actual cooking time is about 5 minutes.

Cooking Time: 5 minutes To serve: 6

INGREDIENTS	METRIC	IMPERIAL	AMERICAN
Oil	40 ml	3 tbsp	3 tbsp
Fish fillets (Any white, non-oily fish will do. Dover or lemon sole work very well.) 1 fillet per person			
Unsalted butter	75 g	3 oz	1/3 cup
Dry white wine	85 ml	6 tbsp	6 tbsp
Chicken stock	85 ml	6 tbsp	6 tbsp
FOR THE VEGETABLE GARNISH:			
Carrots	100 g	4 oz	1 cup
Onion	100 g	4 oz	1 cup
Unsalted butter	50 g	1¾ oz	3 tbsp
Button mushrooms sliced	100 g	4 oz	1 cup
Salt and freshly ground black pepper to taste			
Fresh tarragon, chopped	5 g	1 tsp	1 tsp
(If using dried, use half the amount.)			

FOR PAPILLOTES:
6 rounds of greaseproof paper, or aluminium foil, cut in 30 cm/12 in circles.
Pre-heat the oven to 240°C/475°F/gas mark 9.

To make the garnish
Cut the vegetables for the garnish in julienne strips about the size of a matchstick. If you have a food processor this can be done with a blade made to cut large julienne. (I like to use the blade made for cutting chips.) Place the butter

A papillote made of greaseproof paper

in a frying pan and add the carrots, onions and a little salt and pepper, cover and cook gently for 5 minutes. Then add the mushrooms and cook, covered for 3 more minutes. Add the tarragon and cook covered for a further 2 minutes. Cool.

To make the papillotes
Brush the centre of each paper with oil. Spoon the vegetables into the paper rounds. Place one portion of fish in each round. Put a few leaves of tarragon on the fish. Put a small nut of butter,

Opening the papillote

Poisson en Papillote

1 tablespoon of wine and 1 tablespoon of stock on each paper. Sprinkle with a little salt and pepper. Close the papillotes and seal the edges. For foil, bend them over and press together. For greaseproof paper, fold the edges round the semi-circle overlapping the previous fold as you go. The illustrations above show how the finished papillote should look.

Brush a baking tray with oil and place the papillotes on the tray. Do not overlap. Bake for 4–5 minutes. The fish is done when it is no longer translucent.

To serve
Place each papillote on an individual plate and let your guests open their own. Or, lift the fish and vegetables onto each plate and pour the sauce over them.

HINT: When I make this recipe for several people, I usually make one large papillote and place all the ingredients in it. I then serve them onto the individual plates. This saves time and oven space.

LOTTE À LA NAGE
Monkfish in Light Wine Sauce

A few years ago, people rarely heard of monkfish. Today it has come back into popular use and for good reason. It is a firm-fleshed fish without small bones. It has only one large bone that runs down the centre of the fish. The flesh is very similar to lobster meat and is sometimes used as a substitute. It is rich and meaty and useful in many recipes.

Cooking time: about 20 minutes To serve: 6

INGREDIENTS	METRIC	IMPERIAL	AMERICAN
Onions	2 large	2 large	2 large
Celery	4 stalks	4 stalks	4 stalks
Carrots	4 large	4 large	4 large
Leeks, whites only	6	6	6
Unsalted butter	100 g	4 oz	½ cup
Bay leaves	2	2	2
White wine	450 ml	16 fl oz	2 cups
Fish fumet (stock)	450 ml	16 fl oz	2 cups
Double cream	450 ml	16 fl oz	2 cups
Monkfish, (or any firm white meat fish) skinned and cut into 20 mm/¾ in cubes.	900 g	2 lb	2 lb
Salt and freshly ground black pepper to taste			
TO GARNISH:			
Carrots	4	4	4
Mange tout, (or green beans)	225 g	½ lb	½ lb
Unsalted butter	25 g	1 oz	2 tbsp

HINT: Fish fumet can be made by simmering together fish bones, 1 carrot, sliced, 1 onion, sliced, 1 bay leaf, a few stalks of parsley, 2 branches thyme, 6 peppercorns and enough water to cover the bones. Simmer for 20 minutes. Strain the stock and reduce it to the required amount.

To prepare the sauce
Thinly slice the onions, celery, carrots and leeks. Melt the butter in a heavy-bottomed casserole and sweat all the vegetables. Sauté them for 1 minute and add the bay leaves and a few drops of water. Cover with a piece of greaseproof paper and a lid and sweat until soft. After about 10 minutes, check to see if they are dry. If so, add more water. Sweat for another 5 minutes. In a second pan reduce the wine and fish fumet by half. Add the cream and reduce by half again. Take out the bay leaves and add the cream and fish fumet. Let simmer for 5 minutes. Strain the sauce. The recipe can be made ahead to this point.

To prepare the garnish
Peel the carrots and cut 12 mm/½ in slices on the diagonal. Sauté in butter in a separate pan for 5 minutes. Tip, tail and string the mange tout and add to the carrots. Sauté for 1 more minute.

To cook the fish
Bring the sauce to a simmer and add the fish cubes. Simmer for 2–5 minutes. Do not over-cook the fish. It will be a milky colour when cooked. Add salt and pepper and taste for seasoning.

To serve
Pour the fish and sauce into a shallow serving bowl and add the vegetables, arranging them to show their colour. Serve immediately. The sauce can be made ahead and the fish and vegetables prepared for cooking. The vegetables for the garnish should be crisp, so they are best made at the last minute.

Lotte à la Nage

GOUJONNETTES DE POISSON

Fish Fillets in Cream Sauce

This can be served as a first or main course. Most of it can be prepared in advance and the actual cooking of the fish takes about 2 minutes.

Cooking time: about 10 minutes To serve: 6

INGREDIENTS	METRIC	IMPERIAL	AMERICAN
Fresh mussels	900 g	2 lbs	2 lbs
Freshly ground black pepper			
Fish fillets (any white fish, Dover sole, lemon sole, plaice, monkfish)	900 g	2 lbs	2 lbs
Juice from 1 lemon			
Salt			
Single cream	175 ml	6 oz	¾ cup
Fresh tarragon, finely chopped	5 g	3 tbsp	3 tbsp
(If using dried tarragon, then use half the amount. Dried herbs are stronger.)			
Potato flour or arrowroot, optional	5 g	1 tsp	1 tsp
Cold water, optional	25 ml	1 oz	2 tbsp
Sprigs of fresh tarragon to garnish			

To prepare the mussels

Clean the mussels by taking any bits of the beard off and washing under cold water. The beards are the thin filaments used by the mussel to attach itself to rocks.

HINT: If while washing, you find any mussels that are open, tap them on a counter, if they do not close, discard them.

Place in a heavy-bottomed pan with a lid. Do not add any liquid. Sprinkle with some freshly ground pepper. Place the pan over a medium heat and shake the pan every few minutes to cook the mussels evenly. The mussels will open and their juice will become the base of the sauce. This should take 3–4 minutes. Take off the lid and see if they have opened. Discard any that refuse to open. Remove the mussels from their shells and set aside.

To prepare the fish

Remove any bits of skin or bone from the fillets and cut them into goujonnettes. These are strips about 1.2 cm/½ in wide and 2.5 cm/1 in long. Sprinkle the fish with lemon juice and salt and pepper. Wrap in cling film and set aside until the fish fumet is ready.

To finish the sauce

Strain the mussel juice very carefully. Do not pour the juice; lift it out with a ladle, thus leaving any sand on the bottom. In another pan bring the mussel juice and cream to a light simmer. Add the tarragon, a little salt and pepper, and taste for seasoning. Add more if necessary. This dish can be made ahead to this point. Just bring the sauce to a simmer a few minutes before you are ready to serve and cook the fish.

To cook the fish

Heat the sauce gently in a saucepan and add the fish and mussels. Let the sauce simmer slowly for 1–2 minutes. It should simmer just to cook the fish. When the fish has turned a milky colour, it is done.

HINT: If you prefer a thicker sauce, mix the potato flour with the water and stir into the sauce as it is cooking the fish.

To serve

Pour into serving dish, decorate with sprigs of fresh tarragon, and serve immediately.

Goujonettes de Poisson

SAUCE NEWBURG
Newburg Sauce

This is a very good sauce to serve with fish. It is easily made and can be made in advance and re-warmed. Use it to accompany *Pain de Poisson*.

Cooking time: 5–10 minutes To serve: 8

INGREDIENTS	METRIC	IMPERIAL	AMERICAN
Butter	50 g	2 oz	¼ cup
Plain flour	40 g	1½ oz	3 tbsp
Paprika	5 g	1 tsp	1 tsp
Fish stock	425 ml	15 oz	2 cups
Sherry	50 ml	2 fl oz	¼ cup
Single cream	150 ml	5 fl oz	⅔ cup
Salt and freshly ground white pepper to taste			
TO GARNISH:			
Small shrimps	225 g	8 oz	2 cups

Melt the butter in a saucepan and add the flour and paprika. Cook for a minute to cook the flour and bring out the flavour of the paprika. Blend in the stock to make a smooth sauce. Simmer for a minute. Add the sherry and cream. Add the salt and pepper. Taste for seasoning and add more sherry or salt and pepper if needed.

To serve
Add the shrimps to the warm sauce and serve.

PAIN DE POISSON

This most unusual dish has no translation. It is not a bread but when it is served, it has the appearance of a round bread. The recipe is similar to that for a quenelle and its light texture is a delight. You should find this a wonderful dish for large groups. It is made in a soufflé dish, but can also be made in individual ramekins and served as a first course.

Cooking time: about 1 hour To serve: 8–10

INGREDIENTS	METRIC	IMPERIAL	AMERICAN
Light white fish fillets (pike, haddock, whiting, hake or codling may be used)	340 g	¾ lb	¾ lb
Eggs, lightly beaten	2	2	2
Egg white	1	1	1
Single cream	25 ml	2 tbsp	2 tbsp
Freshly ground nutmeg (or powdered) to taste	10 g	about 2 tsp	about 2 tsp
Salt and freshly ground black pepper to taste			
FOR PANADE:			
Butter	50 g	2 oz	¼ cup
Milk	210 ml	7½ fl oz	scant cup
Plain flour	40 g	1½ oz	2½ tbsp
TO GARNISH: SAUCE NEWBURG			
Soufflé dish 19 cm/6½ in in diameter and 7.5 cm/ 3 in deep prepared with: greaseproof paper and			
Butter	25 g	1 oz	2 tbsp

Pre-heat the oven to 190°C/375°F/gas mark 5

To prepare the soufflé dish
Cut a round of greaseproof paper to fit the bottom of the dish. Generously grease the dish with butter. Place the paper in the bottom and grease the paper.

To make the panade
Melt the butter in the milk and then bring the milk to the boil. (Do not boil the milk before all the butter had melted.) When it is at a rolling boil, take off the heat and quickly pour all the flour in at once. This is easiest done by placing the flour on a piece of paper which can serve as a funnel. Beat well until smooth. This can be hard work, and may be done in a food processor. Cool the panade.

To prepare the fish
Cut the fish into 2.5 cm/1 in cubes and chop finely. Again, this can easily be done in a food

Pain de Poisson avec Sauce Newburg

processor, or the fish can be ground in a food mill using first a coarse blade and then a medium blade. Add the cooled panade to the fish and mix well. Add the eggs, egg white and cream. Add the nutmeg, salt and pepper. It should be well seasoned. Taste and add more seasoning as needed. Turn into the buttered dish.

To cook

Cut a round of greaseproof paper to fit the top of the dish. Butter it and cover the top of the dish. Place the dish in a roasting tin and three-quarters fill the tin with boiling water.

> *HINT: It is best to place the tin and dish in the oven and then bring the kettle to the oven. This avoids trying to carry a roasting tin full of hot water.*

Place in the oven. Bake for 50 minutes. To test if it is ready, stick a knife into the centre, if it comes out clean, then it is done. This method of testing is the same as that for testing a cake.

To finish and serve

Take out of the oven and slide a knife around the edges to release. Turn the dish upside down onto a serving plate and unmould. Remove the greaseproof paper. Pour some of the sauce over the top and round the sides. Serve the rest in a sauce boat.

MOULES À LA MARINIÈRE

Mussels in White Wine Sauce

This dish reminds me of eating by the seaside in France with the sun shining, the fresh smell of the sea filling the air, and a French waiter pouring a chilled glass of white wine. What a treat! Mussels are easy to prepare, very inexpensive to serve, and rarely cooked at home. I hope this recipe will help to change that.

Cooking time: 10–15 minutes To serve: 6–8

INGREDIENTS	METRIC	IMPERIAL	AMERICAN
Mussels	2.7 kg	6 lbs	6 lbs
Unsalted butter	50 g	2 oz	¼ cup
Onions, sliced	2 large	2 large	2 large
Carrots, in thick slices	2	2	2
Sticks of celery, in thick slices	2	2	2
Dry white wine	350 ml	12 fl oz	1½ cups
Freshly ground black pepper to taste			
Fresh parsley, chopped	175 g	6 oz	¾ cup

To prepare the mussels

Wash the mussels carefully under cold water. Scrape off the beard or thin hairs along the shell. This is how the mussel attaches itself to rocks. The mussels should be clean, but you will not be able to scrape off every barnacle and this is not necessary. If any mussels are open, tap them gently. Discard any that do not close. If you have time, place them in a bucket of cold water for an hour. This allows them to clean themselves of sand. Some people like to sprinkle a spoonful of flour or oatmeal over the water for the mussels to feed on, thus disgorging sand in the process. When ready to use, lift the mussels out of the water instead of pouring the water off. This will help to leave the sand behind.

To prepare the sauce

Melt the butter in a large saucepan. Sauté the onions, carrots and celery until they start to shrivel but not colour. This may take 10 minutes. Add the white wine and some freshly ground pepper. Add the mussels and cover tightly. Bring the liquid to the boil. Let boil for about 1 minute. The wine will boil up over the mussels and they will open. As soon as they are open, take off the heat. Do not overcook. The mussels will taste like rubber if you do. Discard any mussels that do not open.

To finish and serve

With a slotted spoon, lift the mussels out of the pan and place in a large serving bowl. Bring the liquid to a boil and reduce rapidly by half. Sprinkle the parsley into the sauce. Pour the sauce over the mussels, leaving about 6 mm/¼ in of the sauce in the pan. This will have some sand in it. Serve immediately.

The vegetables can be sautéd in advance and the mussels cooked just before serving.

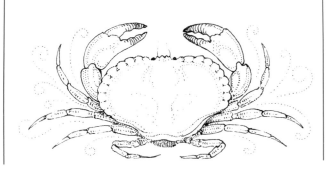

SAUCE MAYONNAISE
Mayonnaise

Mayonnaise is an emulsion. One fat, oil, is suspended in another, egg yolk. Certain rules must be followed in order to achieve the desired suspension. It is very simple to make, especially with an electric mixer or food processor and will last for at least a week or more in the refrigerator. I find it tastes nicer than bought preparations.

General Rules:
1 One egg yolk will accept about 150–175 ml/ 5–6 fl oz/½–¾ cup of oil. If too much oil is added, the mixture will break down (curdle).
2 The egg yolk should be prepared to receive the oil. This is done by beating the yolk thoroughly before any oil is added.
3 The oil must be added to the yolk very slowly so that the yolk will be able to absorb the oil.
4 For the best results the egg yolk and oil should be at room temperature.

Preparation time: 10 minutes

INGREDIENTS	METRIC	IMPERIAL	AMERICAN
Egg yolk	1	1	1
Mustard	2.5 ml	½ tsp	½ tsp
Salt and freshly ground black pepper to taste			
Oil (corn oil, sunflower oil, olive oil)	150 ml	5 fl oz	5 fl oz
Wine vinegar or lemon juice	20 ml	½ tbsp	½ tbsp

Beat the egg yolk, add the mustard and add a little salt and pepper (about 1 teaspoon of salt). When the yolk is creamy, add the oil drop by drop, beating constantly. As the mayonnaise begins to thicken, the oil can be added at a faster pace. When nearly all the oil has been added, pour in the vinegar and finish with the oil, beating constantly. Taste for seasoning.

HINTS: 1 If your mixture curdles, do not throw it away. Start with another egg yolk and add the curdled mixture drop by drop as you did for the oil above.
2 This mayonnaise will keep at least a week in the refrigerator.
3 Varying types of herbs and oils may be added to this recipe giving different types of sauces.
4 This recipe can be made in a food processor or with an electric beater. Mayonnaise made in a blender is based on a different recipe and has a different texture.

SAUCE VINAIGRETTE
Vinaigrette

Preparation time: 3 minutes

INGREDIENTS	METRIC	IMPERIAL	AMERICAN
Wine vinegar	25 ml	2 tbsp	2 tbsp
Mustard	10 ml	2 tsp	2 tsp
Oil (corn, sunflower, olive, walnut, hazelnut or any combination you wish)	175 ml	6 fl oz	¾ cup
Salt and freshly ground black pepper to taste (about ½ tsp)			

Whisk the mustard and vinegar together thoroughly. Be sure they are well mixed. Add salt and pepper to taste. Pour in the oil and whisk again. Taste for seasoning. It should have a creamy texture.

HINT: If your mixture separates, this means that the mustard and vinegar were not thoroughly blended before the oil was added. Sometimes you can bring it back together by processing it in a food processor with an ice cube. If it is too far gone for this trick, then start with more vinegar and mustard, mixed well and slowly add the separated mixture. Adjust the seasoning.

CRABE FARCI
Stuffed Crab

Crab is elegant and delicious to serve. Crabs are in season throughout the summer months and sometimes through to Christmas. They can be brought ready-cooked from your fishmonger or are easy to cook yourself. This dish is served cold and makes a wonderful buffet dish or after-theatre supper.

Preparation time: 20 minutes To serve: 6

INGREDIENTS	METRIC	IMPERIAL	AMERICAN
Crabs (3 ½ lb/1.5 kg each)	3	3	3
Bread crumbs	65 g	5 tbsp	5 tbsp
Vinaigrette (page 75)	25–40 ml	2–3 tbsp	2–3 tbsp
Mayonnaise (page 75)	40–70 ml	3–5 tbsp	3–5 tbsp
Oil	25 ml	2 tbsp	2 tbsp
Salt and freshly ground black pepper to taste			
Fresh parsley, finely chopped	45 g	3 tbsp	3 tbsp
FOR GARNISH:			
Head of lettuce, washed, dried	1	1	1

HINT: Make sure the crabs are fresh. The best ones are still warm from having just been cooked.

To cook your own crab
Place the crab in a pan of warm water. Bring the water to the boil and simmer for about 15 minutes per pound. Do not bring to a heavy boil. The meat will become rubbery if you do. Pull the shell off the main body to open and take out the feathery lungs and small sac. These are located just under the head and are together.

To prepare the cooked crab
When you buy your crab cooked, ask the fishmonger to open it and discard the lungs and sac.

Opening up the crab

Taking out the lungs and sac

When the crab is opened it will be in two parts: one is the shell, the other is the main body with the legs attached. Take off the large and small claws and set aside. Scrape out all the brown creamy meat from the shell and place in a bowl. There will be a wavy line along the shell. Tap it firmly with crab and lobster crackers, and the shell will break back to this line. Wash the shell and oil it. Set aside. Rinse the small claws and oil. Set aside. Crack the large claws, extract the meat and place it in a second bowl. Shred the meat. Break the honeycombed body in two and with a skewer take out all the white meat. Be careful not to get any of the fine white shell in the meat. It is very difficult to keep all the shell

Scraping out the brown meat from the shell

Taking the white meat out of the body

Tapping the shell with lobster crackers to take it back the wavy line

Crabe Farci served with champagne

out of the meat. After you have extracted all the meat, run your finger tips through the meat, taking out any bits of shell as you find them.

To prepare the meat

Add the bread crumbs and some of the vinaigrette to the dark meat, to bind it together. Mix well and add more vinaigrette if necessary. Taste for seasoning and add salt and pepper as needed. Add half the mayonnaise to the white meat. Add more mayonnaise to bind together if necessary. Taste for seasoning and add salt and pepper as needed.

To assemble

Place the dark meat in a line down the centre of the shell, across the width. Try to make it a neat and smooth line. Spoon the white meat into the shell on either side of the dark meat. Very carefully sprinkle a thin line of chopped parsley in two rows separating the white meat from the dark meat.

To make the chiffonade

Take the lettuce leaves and roll them up, like a cigar. With a sharp knife, thinly slice the cigar shape.

To serve

Place the chiffonade on a large round serving platter. Place the crab on the chiffonade and arrange the claws around the crab. Serve with slices of toast or biscuits.

LA VOLAILLE
POULTRY

'I want each of my peasants to have a chicken in his pot on Sunday.'

Much time has passed since Henry IV of France made this famous statement. Modern chicken farming has made this dish of nobles available to us all. By carefully selecting the correct type of bird for each recipe, delectable results can be achieved.

There are many styles of serving poultry. Boned and stuffed, it can be the highlight of the most elegant of dinners. Roasting or grilling results in a less elaborate presentation. Cooking very slowly in a sauce imparts the flavours of the vegetables or herbs cooked with it. Whichever way you choose, it should always be popular and enjoyed.

The presence of duck on any menu signifies something special and exciting to come. It is a rich and more luxurious bird than chicken and needs careful cooking. Many of us choose to enjoy duck in a restaurant rather than attempting to cook it at home, but this should not be necessary. Served with a very crisp skin with all the fat cooked away and juicy tender meat, it is certainly a treat.

Today's emphasis on low fat meats provides an incentive to find new ways of serving the traditional poultry dinner. In the following pages, I hope you will discover some that you find exciting and enticing.

To start with, I would like you to be aware of the varieties of poultry available. Choosing the best fresh poultry available is the start of any successful dish.

Chicken is a generic term that describes anything from a new born chick to a large fowl. Duck is classified by its type and age. Below is a chart to help you recognise the type of bird used in my recipes.

Poussin	3–4 weeks old young and tender, not much flavour
Spring Chicken	chicken up to 3 lbs, used for most recipes, mature but not fatty
Roasting Chicken	chicken from 3–4 lbs, good for rôtisserie or grill
Poulard	chicken 4–4¼ lbs, used for stews
Duckling	under 6 months, best for roasting, weighs 4–5 lbs.
Duck	over 6 months, rarely used. It is uneconomical to farm ducks longer than 6 months, thus they are brought to market at this time or earlier.

General Hints on preparation
Poultry should be trussed when cooked. This not only helps to hold the shape, but also brings the thighs up to the breast to protect this delicate meat.

To test whether a bird is done, stick a knife into the thigh area. If the juices run clear, they are done, if they run red or pink let the bird cook longer.

Ducks seem to change in texture and flavour when frozen. I prefer only to use fresh ducks.

Ducks are in season all year round, but are best in June and July. Try to choose one with a plump breast.

POULETTE AU VINAIGRE DE XÉRÈS
Chicken with Sherry Wine Vinegar

Vinegar has come into vogue as a creative ingredient in *nouvelle cuisine* recipes. Raspberry, cherry, fennel and tarragon vinegars are a few of the many available. The list goes on and on. It's great fun to try out different vinegars. In this case, vinegar gives the flavour to an unusual sauce. Sherry wine vinegar can be found in most delicatessens today and keeps a very long time on the shelf.

Cooking time: approximately 30 minutes To serve: 4

INGREDIENTS	METRIC	IMPERIAL	AMERICAN
Butter	25 g	1 oz	2 tbsp
Chicken, quartered	1.4 kg	3 lbs	3 lbs
Sherry wine vinegar	40–50 ml	3–4 tbsp	3–4 tbsp
Garlic, unpeeled	3 cloves	3 cloves	3 cloves
Chicken stock	225 ml	8 fl oz	1 cup
Crème fraîche	225 ml	8 fl oz	1 cup
TO GARNISH:			
Castor sugar to sprinkle on top of the chicken			

Heat the butter in a heavy-bottomed casserole and sauté the chicken pieces until they are golden brown (about 10 minutes). Pour off the excess fat and sprinkle 1 tablespoon of sherry wine vinegar over them. Add the garlic cloves. Cover and gently simmer over low heat for 5 minutes. Add another tablespoon of the vinegar and simmer, covered, for another 5 minutes.

Sprinkle one more tablespoon of vinegar over the chicken and cook for another 5 minutes. Take out the white meat and cook the dark meat for another 5 minutes. Check to see that the chicken is done. If it is not ready, cook for another 5 minutes.

Take out the chicken and add the stock to the juices in the pan. Turn up the heat and reduce the liquid by half, leaving the casserole uncovered. Mash the garlic and add the crème fraîche. Taste for seasoning. Add salt and pepper as necessary. It may need 2 more teaspoons of the vinegar. Strain the sauce.

To serve
Sprinkle a little sugar on the chicken and crisp it under the grill. Serve with the sauce. This dish can be made earlier in the day and kept in a warm place. In this case, re-warm under the grill just before it is served.

POULET AUX CHAMPIGNONS
Chicken with Mushrooms

This chicken dish with its sherry and mushroom sauce is a favourite because it can be put on to cook and forgotten about. An hour later the chicken with a lovely sauce is ready to serve. Because the chicken is gently sweated, it remains moist and can be easily re-warmed.

(Eight equal pieces are carved off a chicken. Usually 2 per person is enough. Determine your own count and adjust the other ingredients for the number of chickens)

Cooking time: about one hour To serve: 4

INGREDIENTS	METRIC	IMPERIAL	AMERICAN
Salt and freshly ground black pepper to taste			
Spring chicken	1.1–1.4 kg	2½–3 lb	2½–3 lb
Lemon	½	½	½
Butter	25 g	1 oz	2 tbsp
Garlic, crushed	1 clove	1 clove	1 clove
Sherry	120 ml	4 oz	½ cup
Wild mushrooms, fresh or dried	50 g	2 fl oz	½ cup
Button mushrooms	225 g	8 oz	2 cups
TO GARNISH:			
Crème fraîche	15–25 ml	1–2 tbs	1–2 tbs

Salt and pepper the inside of the chicken and truss, or at least tie the legs together. Rub the chicken with the half lemon. Place the butter in a casserole just large enough to fit the chicken. (If it is too large the juices will run along the bottom and evaporate.) Place over a low heat. When the butter has melted, turn the chicken in it and add the garlic and sherry. Cover tightly and cook slowly for about 1 hour turning from time to time.

HINT: Sherry has a high sugar content. If it is cooked on a high flame it will burn easily.

In the meantime soak the wild mushrooms in boiling water, if they are dried. Wash and quarter the button mushrooms. Add the mushrooms to the chicken 10 minutes before the end of cooking and continue to simmer. Test the chicken to see if it is ready. If not, cook for 10 minutes longer. Take the chicken out and joint or carve and place on a warm serving dish. Stir a spoonful of crème fraîche into the juices in the casserole. Add salt and pepper to taste.

To serve
Pour some of the sauce and mushrooms over the carved chicken and serve the rest in a sauce boat.

Poulet au Champignons

BALLOTINE DE VOLAILLE
Boned Stuffed Chicken

This is a special and elegant party dish. The chicken can be boned and stuffed in advance, and frozen. It can then be taken out and cooked the day before it is needed. When the ballotine is finished, about 30 slices can be carved.

Many butchers will bone the poultry for you if you order it in advance. However, if you find yourself in front of a chicken waiting to be boned, don't worry. It's really easier than it seems. Try to use the step-by-step instructions. Your first attempt may take some time but subsequent tries will take no more than 20 minutes.

Boning a Chicken

1. The important thing when boning a chicken is to understand just where the bones lie. Start along the backbone and run the knife down the backbone from the neck to the tail, with the knife edge cutting against the bone.

2. Slip your knife under the skin and flesh and work around to the front, always scraping your knife against the bones, ending at the breast bone. When you come to the joints connecting the wings and legs to the carcass, sever them, separating them from the carcass, but leaving them attached to the meat. Repeat the process on the other side.

3. The chicken meat will fall away from the carcass, remaining attached at the breast bone. Very carefully cut against the ridge of the breast bone to separate the carcass and the meat completely. Be careful not to slit the skin. The body of the chicken will be separate from the bones, leaving the legs and wings attached.

1.

2.

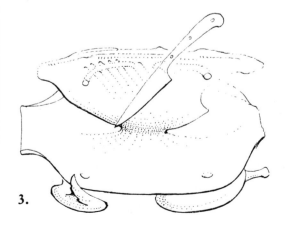

3.

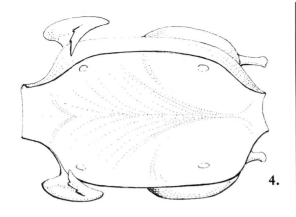

4. Cut off the wings at the 'elbow' joint and scrape the meat from the wing bones. Cut off the legs at the joint below the thigh and scrape the meat from the remaining bones. The chicken may look like a mass of skin and meat to you at this point, but if you lay it out flat on the counter in front of you, a rectangular shape will appear. Pull the wing meat and leg meat inside out, similar to the sleeve of a coat.

5. and **6.** Now you are ready to stuff the chicken, but first make the sauce brune.

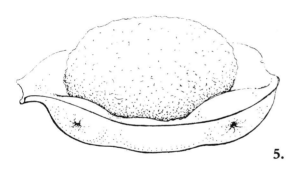

4.

5.

SAUCE BRUNE

Brown Sauce

Cooking time: about 30–40 minutes. To make approximately 7 fl oz

INGREDIENTS	METRIC	IMPERIAL	AMERICAN
Butter	25 g	1 oz	2 tbsp
Onion, carrot, celery, diced together measuring	25 g	2 tbsp	2 tbsp
Flour	15 g	½ oz	1 tbsp
Brown stock	300 ml	10 fl oz	1¼ cup
Tomato purée (paste)	5 ml	1 tsp	1 tsp
Mushroom trimmings	5 g	2 tsp	2 tsp

Bouquet garni (a few springs of thyme, parsley stalks, and 1 bay leaf tied together with kitchen string).

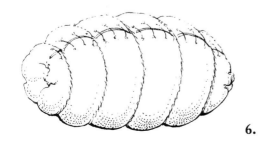

6.

Warm the butter in a heavy-bottomed saucepan. Add the vegetables and cook gently until they shrivel but do not colour. Add the flour and cook very slowly until a russet brown colour. Cool a little. Pour in the stock all at once, saving about 30 ml/2 fl oz/¼ cup for later. Stir until simmering. Add the tomato purée, mushrooms, bouquet garni and simmer for 20–25 minutes with the lid half on. Strain into a clean pan. Bring to the boil and add the reserved stock. Scum will come to the top as the sauce comes back to the boil. Skim it off. Taste for seasoning.

*Ballotine de Volaille avec Pommes de Terre à la
Vapeur (p 123) et Julienne de Courgettes et de Carottes
(p 118)*

To prepare the Ballotiine

Now the boned chicken and sauce brune are ready, you can stuff the chicken.

Cooking time: 1–1½ hours To serve: 8–10

INGREDIENTS	METRIC	IMPERIAL	AMERICAN
Spring chicken, boned (page 82)	1.4 kg	3 lb	3 lb
FOR FARCE:			
Onion, chopped	1 large	1 large	1 large
Butter	25 g	1 oz	2 tbsp
Minced veal	225 g	8 oz	8 oz
Minced pork	225 g	8 oz	8 oz
Fresh sage, chopped	20 g	1½ tbsp	1½ tbsp
Fresh parsley, chopped	25 g	2 tbsp	2 tbsp
Pecans, or pistachios, or walnuts, coarsely chopped	50 g	2 oz	½ cup
Egg	1	1	1
Salt and freshly ground black pepper to taste			
FOR THE SAUCE:			
Chicken stock	300 ml	10 fl oz	1¼ cups
Red wine	300 ml	10 fl oz	1¼ cups
Sauce brune (page 83)	200 ml	7 fl oz	scant cup

To make farce

Sweat the onion in butter until transparent. Mix together all the ingredients, including the onions, for the farce. Be sure to season well. Take a small bit of the farce and sauté it. Taste this piece and correct the seasoning if necessary.

To fill the chicken

Open the chicken out flat, and salt and pepper the flesh side. Place the stuffing in the middle running in a line down the centre.

HINT: Do not overfill with the farce. It will expand during cooking and ooze into the sauce.

Bring the chicken together and sew with kitchen string. Shape it into a sausage and tie string in circles around the sausage to help keep its shape.

(The ballotine can be frozen at this point. Place in a strong polythene bag. Take out 24 hours before you are ready to use it and let it thaw in the refrigerator.)

To cook

Brown the chicken in a heavy-bottomed casserole. Add about 2.5 cm/1 in of chicken stock. Cook, covered for 1½ hours in the oven at 170°C/325°F/gas mark 3, or simmer on a hob. Turn the chicken over once or twice while cooking. When done, take out and place in a tin with a weight on it for at least 15 minutes.

HINT: The easiest way to weight the ballotine is to place it in a large loaf tin, place some foil over it and fill a bag with some beans or rice and place on top. Failing this, if you don't have weights in the kitchen, use a heavy tin.

You can leave the chicken in the refrigerator for several hours, or overnight. While the chicken is resting, make the sauce.

To make the sauce

Take all the fat off the cooking liquid and add enough stock to make 300 ml/½ pt/1¼ cups. This may require more or less stock than indicated above, depending upon the amount of juice given off by the chicken. Add the wine and reduce the mixture by half, by boiling it rapidly. Add the sauce brune. Taste, and add more salt and pepper if necessary. Strain the sauce and serve with the chicken.

To serve

Thinly slice the ballotine and lay the slices overlapping on a serving plate. If this has been made in advance, pour a little of the sauce over the chicken to keep it moist and cover with foil. Heat gently in the oven just to warm through. Serve the rest of the sauce in a gravy boat.

This ballotine is also delicious served cold at a buffet or for a picnic. For the best flavour serve at room temperature, not just out of the fridge. Omit the sauce.

POUSSIN À LA DIJONNAISE

Poussin with Dijon Mustard Sauce

The sweet and pungent taste created by the mixture of orange juice and mustard is an unusual and pleasant combination. The delicate young birds are gently steamed which keeps them tender and juicy. This is a good dish for making in advance and finishing just before serving.

Cooking time: approximately 30 minutes To serve: 6

INGREDIENTS	METRIC	IMPERIAL	AMERICAN
Poussins (count ½ poussin per person)	3	3	3
Butter	70 g	2½ oz	¼ cup + 1 tbsp
Chicken stock	175 ml	6 fl oz	¾ cup
Salt	5 g	1 tsp	1 tsp
Fresh ground black pepper to taste			
Dijon mustard	20 g	1½ tbsp	1½ tbsp
Orange zest, (grated rind), a few peelings and juice from orange	1	1	1
Double cream	25 ml	2 tbsp	2 tbsp
TO GARNISH:			
Castor sugar	40–50 g	3–4 tbsp	3–4 tbsp
Watercress	1 bunch	1 bunch	1 bunch

Salt and pepper the inside of the poussins and add the peel from one orange. Truss the birds or tie the legs together.

Melt the butter in a casserole just large enough to fit the birds snugly. If it is too large the juices will run over the bottom and evaporate. Turn the birds over in the butter to coat and add the stock, salt and pepper. Cover and bring to the boil. Lower the heat and simmer gently for about 20–25 minutes. This should be enough time for these small birds.

HINT: Try not to cook over a high heat. Any protein that is heavily boiled will become rubbery.

Test the birds to see that they are done. If they are not ready, cook for 5–10 minutes longer. Place the birds on a carving board and cut in half. With a poultry shears or knife cut out the back bone and take off the pinions (tip of the wing). Arrange the halves on a greased serving tray that can go under a grill.

Make the sauce by adding the mustard and zest of orange and half of the juice to the casserole. Add the cream and taste for salt and pepper or perhaps more orange juice or mustard. You should be able to taste each flavour without being overpowered by one. Add more if necessary. Strain the sauce into a clean saucepan. The recipe can be prepared in advance up to this point.

Just before serving, brush the birds with some melted butter and the rest of the orange juice. Sprinkle with the sugar. Place under a hot grill to caramelise the sugar and crisp the skin. The birds should be a golden brown colour. Taste the sauce. It may need more seasoning after resting for a while. Heat it gently.

HINT: Orange juice can become bitter if boiled.

To serve

Pour some of the sauce around the poussins, but not on top or the skin will lose its crispness. Decorate with a bouquet of watercress placed on one side of the dish.

CANARD À L'ORANGE
Duck in Orange Sauce

One of the most traditional of all French dishes. If your brown sauce is prepared ahead, the duck can be roasted, and the entire dish put together very quickly.

Cooking time: duck 1 hour, finishing the sauce 10 min To serve: 6

INGREDIENTS	METRIC	IMPERIAL	AMERICAN
2 ducks, each weighing	1.6–1.8 kg	3½–4 lb	3½–4 lb
Salt and freshly ground pepper to taste			
Orange peelings and juice from orange	1	1	1
Butter	50 g	2 oz	¼ cup
Red wine	175 ml	6 oz	¾ cup
Redcurrant jelly, creamed	25–40 g	2–3 tbsp	2–3 tbsp
Sauce Brune (page 83)	200 ml	7 fl oz	scant cup
TO GARNISH:			
Orange needle shreds and segments from oranges			

Pre-heat the oven to 200°C/400°F/gas mark 6

To roast the duck

Remove all of the fat from the cavity of the ducks. Salt and pepper the cavity and place a few orange peelings inside. Truss, or at least tie the legs together to help keep the shape. Rub butter over the skin. Prick the skin all over, especially around the thighs and breast, to allow the fat just under the skin to drain off as it cooks. Place on a rack in a roasting tin and roast for about 1 hour. Every 20 minutes take the pan out and draw off the fat. This will keep it from spattering in your oven. The French like their ducks medium rare. The juices will run slightly pink rather than clear. If you like your duck more well done, then roast it for 1 hour 20 minutes. The juices will run clear. Don't overcook the duck, however, otherwise it will be dry and a little like cardboard.

While the duck is roasting make the orange needle shreds and segments.

To make the shreds

These can be made in advance and kept in a damp piece of kitchen towel in the refrigerator. With a potato peeler carefully peel off pieces of the skin of the oranges trying not to take any of the white pith. Cut these into needle thin shreds and blanch in boiling water for 1 minute. Rinse in cold water.

To make orange segments

With a serrated fruit knife cut around the skin of the oranges so that there is no pith left. Take the knife and cut between the orange segment and the thin membrane all round the orange.

HINT: Place foil over the duck and let it rest while making the sauce. The juices travel toward the centre during roasting. Letting the bird rest allows time for the juices to flow back through the meat.

To make the sauce

After the duck is removed from the roasting tin, pour off all of the fat. There should be lots of good brown bits on the bottom. Place the roasting tin on a hob and deglaze the pan with the red wine. This is done by scraping all the hardened cooking juices into the wine sauce, adding flavour to the wine. Reduce the juices in the pan by boiling rapidly. Lower the heat and add half the juice from the orange and the redcurrant jelly. Stir until all the jelly is dissolved into the sauce. Strain the juices from the pan and add the sauce brune. This is a delicate blend of flavours, so taste the sauce to see if it needs more jelly or orange juice. Add salt and pepper to taste.

To serve

Carve the duck and pour a little sauce over the meat. Serve the rest in a sauce boat. Sprinkle the needle shreds and segments over the meat. This dish looks very colourful on a dinner party table.

CANARD AU CHOCOLAT
Duck with Chocolate Sauce

Modern French cuisine has brought us some rather strange combinations. From the name you may think this is one of the extremes. However, I assure you that the combination of rich duck meat and tangy sauce is perfect. It's a good party dish because the sauce can be made in advance and served with a freshly roasted duck. The sauce is also very good with game.

Cooking time: 15 mins for the sauce, about 1 hour to roast the duck To serve: 6

INGREDIENTS	METRIC	IMPERIAL	AMERICAN
2 ducks each weighing	1.6–1.8 kg	3½–4 lb	3½–4 lb
Salt and freshly ground pepper to taste			
Butter	50 g	2 oz	¼ cup
FOR THE SAUCE:			
Castor sugar	50 g	4 tbsp	4 tbsp
Water	85 ml	3 fl oz	6 tbsp
Powdered cocoa (not drinking chocolate)	10 g	¾ tbsp	¾ tbsp
Potato flour (corn flour may be substituted)	10 g	¾ tbsp	¾ tbsp
Dry white wine	450 ml	16 fl oz	2 cups
Wine vinegar	25 ml	2 tbsp	2 tbsp
Butter	15 g	½ oz	1 tbsp
Zest of 1 orange (grated rind)			
TO GARNISH:			
Spiced pears, peaches or apricots (found in delicatessens).			

Pre-heat oven to 200°C/400°F/gas mark 6.

To roast the ducks

Remove all the fat from the cavity of the ducks. Salt and pepper the cavity and truss or at least tie the legs together to help keep the shape. Rub butter over the skin and prick the skin all over, especially around the thighs and breast, to allow the fat just under the skin to drain off as it cooks. Place on a rack in a roasting tin and roast for about 1 hour. Every 20 minutes take the pan out and draw off the fat. This will keep it from spattering in your oven. The French like their ducks medium rare. The juices will run slightly pink rather than clear. If you like your duck more well done, then roast it for 1 hour 20 minutes. The juices will run clear. Don't over-cook the duck, however, otherwise it will be dry and a little like cardboard.

HINT: Place foil over the duck and let it rest while making the sauce. The juices travel towards the centre during roasting. Letting the bird rest allows time for the juice to flow back through the meat.

HINT: Have all your ingredients ready to use. You must work quickly when the sugar starts to caramelise. Be careful: use an oven glove or wrap your hand in a tea towel in case the caramel spatters. It can cause a nasty burn.

To make the sauce

Melt the sugar and water in a heavy-bottomed saucepan. Do not bring the liquid to a boil until the sugar is completely dissolved. Boil the sugar solution until a light caramel colour. Remove from the heat. Stir in the cocoa and potato flour, 225 ml/8 fl oz/1 cup of wine and all the wine vinegar.

At this point the mixture will harden slightly. Place back on the heat and stir until it is smooth. Add the butter, the remaining 8 fl oz of wine and the orange rind. Reduce the sauce until it is a smooth, medium thick consistency. It can be made ahead and re-heated. If it becomes too thick on standing, add a little more wine.

To serve

Carve the duck and arrange on a serving platter. Slice the spiced fruit and arrange around the duck. Serve with the sauce.

Canard au Chocolat

LE VEAU
VEAL

Veal is sometimes called 'the chameleon of the kitchen', a quote attributed to Grimond de la Reyniere, an eighteenth century gourmand. The charm of veal seems to be its ability to go with so many flavours and textures. Italians are the world's greatest eaters of veal, using it to show off their culinary abilities. The English, however, seem to eat the least. This may be due to the fact that most veal in England is a by-product of the milk industry and is not specially raised for meat consumption. Thus, the best veal is imported and very expensive.

Veal is an excellent choice for a late evening dinner, or whenever a light meal is in order. With its light texture it will leave your guests satisfied, but without the heavy feeling that comes from richer dishes. It's also one of my favourite choices for an easy dinner. It can be sautéed in minutes or left to slow cook without much attention needed. The meat juices and sauce ingredients are ready with little additional preparation.

Hints on Buying and Cooking Veal

Knowing something about veal production can help you to choose the best veal available to you. Milk fed or as it's sometimes called 'anaemic veal' comes from a calf that is no more than 12 weeks old. After this period it starts to eat grains and grass and the flesh starts to turn pink, and when full grown is red. The best veal comes from a calf 2½-3 months old which has been fed on milk and eggs. The flesh should be firm, smooth, fine-grained and the fat white and satiny.

The best cuts of veal, such as veal escalopes, should not be overcooked. One to three minutes is sufficient.

Usually a light sauce goes best with the better cuts, as this helps to enhance the delicate flavour of the meat.

The cuts for slow cooking do not need as much time to cook as beef. In addition the resulting sauce is less fatty.

Here is a list of the cuts of veal I have used:

Escalopes – The first cut of escalopes comes from either the fillet, or muscles in the leg. The second cut of escalope comes from a muscle in the shoulder called by some butchers, leg of mutton cut. This is usually much less expensive than the first cut, and provides a very good substitute for the first quality.

Leg of mutton cut is also very good for slow cooking. It comes in one piece and weighs generally 1–1.4 kg/2½–3 lb.

Pie veal – usually cut from any part of the veal that is not a large enough size for other uses. It is available in cubes and is reasonably priced.

Veau au Citron
Veal with Lemon Sauce
Cooking time: about 1 hour To serve: 6–8

INGREDIENTS	METRIC	IMPERIAL	AMERICAN
Small button or pickling onions, or the bulbs of spring onions	900 g	2 lb	2 lb
Cloves	6 whole	6 whole	6 whole
Butter	100 g	4 oz	½ cup
Carrots, cut in cubes about the same size as the onions	4 large	4 large	4 large
Oil	25 ml	1 tbsp	1 tbsp
Pie veal cut in 2 in cubes	680–900 g	1½–2 lbs	1½–2 lbs
Flour	40 g	3 tbsp	3 tbsp
Dry white wine	300 ml	½ pt	1¼ cups
Water	200 ml	7 fl oz	scant cup
Juice of 5 lemons			
Garlic, crushed	4 cloves	4 cloves	4 cloves
Bouquet garni (few stalks parsley, 2 branches fresh thyme, 1 bay leaf tied together)			
Tomatoes	3	3	3
Salt and freshly ground black pepper to taste			

Peel the onions or cut the greens and trim the spring onions.

HINT: The easiest way to peel the onions is to blanch them first. Bring water to the boil, add the onions and wait for the water to return to the boil. Drain and plunge into cold water. The skins will then come off easily.

Take the largest 2 onions and stick the 6 cloves in them. Melt 50 g/2 oz/¼ cup butter in a saucepan. Put in the carrots and onions and leave them on a low heat to brown, stirring occasionally.

To prepare the meat
In a heavy-bottomed casserole, heat 50 g/2 oz/ ¼ cup of butter with the oil. Brown the veal. Take out all the meat when browned.

HINT: Each time you put a piece of meat in the pan it lowers the temperature, so if you put all the meat in at once, you will find the meat steaming instead of browning. To avoid this, place 1 or 2 pieces in at a time, after a minute add another piece, thus giving the pan a chance to regain the high temperature needed. Take out the pieces as they brown.

HINT: When sautéing any meat, move it around the pan as soon as it is put in. This avoids sticking.

Take out all the meat.

To cook the casserole
Add the flour to the juices and cook, stirring constantly, until the flour turns straw colour. This is called a roux blond. Add the wine and water, stirring to blend well with the roux. Add three quarters of the lemon juice and taste. Add the rest little by little, watching to see that the sauce doesn't develop too much of an acid flavour. More lemon can be added at the end if needed. Add the garlic, meat, bouquet garni, and the browned onions and carrots. Skin, quarter and de-seed the tomatoes and add to the casserole.

HINT: To peel the tomatoes, blanch by placing in boiling water for 8–12 seconds and plunge into cold water. Then peel.

Bring the liquid to a boil and lower to a simmer. Cook gently for 50 minutes. Stick the point of a knife into a piece of meat to check that it is tender. Taste for seasoning. Add salt, pepper and lemon juice as necessary.

To serve
Take out the bouquet garni and the onions with the cloves. Spoon the meat and vegetables into a warmed serving dish and serve.

SAUTÉ DE VEAU AUX POIREAUX

Sautéed Veal with Leeks

This is an easy casserole dish that lends itself to making in advance and freezing. The leeks, lemon and raisins give it an oriental flavour.

Cooking time: approximately 1 hour 15 mins. To serve: 6

INGREDIENTS	METRIC	IMPERIAL	AMERICAN
Butter	40 g	1½ oz	⅓ cup
Peanut oil (corn oil can be used)	100 ml	3½ fl oz	scant ½ cup
Pie veal, cut into 2 in cubes	800 g	1¾ lbs	1¾ lbs
Leeks, finely sliced	800 g	1¾ lb	1¾ lb
Dry white wine	100 ml	3½ fl oz	3½ fl oz
Milk	200 ml	7 fl oz	7 oz
Bouquet garni (few stalks of parsley, 2 branches fresh thyme, 1 bay leaf tied together)			
Salt and freshly ground pepper to taste			
Raisins or sultanas, washed	40 g	1½ oz	⅓ cup
Lemon juice from ½ lemon			

Heat the oil and butter in a heavy-bottomed casserole. Place all the meat in side by side so that each piece touches the bottom of the casserole. Sauté the meat on a medium-high heat, turning frequently, for about 15 minutes until it is a golden brown colour. Add the leeks and cook for another 10 minutes without colouring them. Add the wine, milk and bouquet garni. Add a little salt and pepper. Simmer gently for 25 minutes. Pierce the meat to check if it is tender. Take out the bouquet garni and add the raisins and lemon juice. Taste for seasoning. Add more salt and pepper if necessary.

To serve

Place in heated serving dish and serve. If made in advance or frozen, rewarm before serving.

ESCALOPES DE VEAU À LA CRÈME

Veal Escalopes in Cream Sauce

This is one of my favourite dishes to make when I've been out all day and friends are coming round for dinner. It takes very little preparation yet, when properly cooked, the sauce appears intricate and sophisticated.

Cooking time: 5–10 minutes To serve: 6

INGREDIENTS	METRIC	IMPERIAL	AMERICAN
Veal escalope (1 per person)	6	6	6
Butter	50 g	2 oz	½ cup
Crème fraîche	80 ml	6 tbsp	6 tbsp
Freshly ground nutmeg to taste			
Salt and freshly ground black pepper to taste			

HINT: When you buy the veal, ask your butcher to bat it out for you. Otherwise, place the meat on a flat surface and bat it out with a meat bat or the bottom of a frying pan. Use a sliding motion rather than straight up and down.

To cook the meat

Place the butter in a sauté pan and when it is hot, place 1 escalope in, moving it around the pan to avoid sticking. When the butter is hot again add another escalope. Turn the first piece over as soon as it is golden. This will take less than 1 minute. Salt and pepper the cooked side. Remove from the pan onto a warmed serving plate. Continue in this way until all the meat is cooked. Remove all the meat from the pan.

To make the sauce

Deglaze the pan with the crème fraîche by pouring the cream in and scraping off all the bits in the pan to incorporate the meat flavour into the cream. Cook for a minute, then add some nutmeg, salt and pepper and taste for seasoning. Add more if necessary. Place the meat back in

the sauce and lower the heat. Cook for about 1 minute. The veal should not cook for more than 1–2 minutes per side in all.

To serve

Place the veal on a serving platter and pour the sauce over it. Serve immediately.

Escalopes de Veau à la Crème (above)

Sauté de Veau aux Poireaux (right)

VEAU À L'ORANGE
Veal in Orange Sauce

This is a lovely, slow-cooked dish with a light *new-wave* sauce. The veal cooks in its marinade and the resulting sauce is very much like a cream sauce, but no cream is used. Instead it is a blend of oranges, lemons and stock.

Cooking time: approximately 1 hour To serve: 6–8

INGREDIENTS	METRIC	IMPERIAL	AMERICAN
1 LMC (leg of mutton cut) of veal	1.4 kg	3 lb	3 lb
FOR THE MARINADE:			
Onion, sliced	1 large	1 large	1 large
Juice of oranges	2	2	2
Juice of lemon	1	1	1
Garlic, bruised to release the juices	1 clove	1 clove	1 clove
Bouquet garni (a few stalks parsley, 2 branches fresh thyme, 1 bay leaf)			
Fresh sprig of basil (if unavailable use 1 tbs/15 g dried)			
FOR THE SAUCE:			
Oil	25 ml	1 fl oz	2 tbsp
Sugar	20 g	4 tsp	4 tsp
White wine vinegar	50 ml	2 fl oz	¼ cup
Chicken stock	85 ml	3 fl oz	6 tbsp
TO GARNISH:			
Needle shreds and orange segments	1	1	1

HINT: A leg of mutton cut is a muscle that is cut from the shoulder of the veal and has nothing to do with mutton. The shape of this muscle is similar to a leg of mutton. It is all one piece of meat. If it is difficult to find, ask your butcher for a slow-cooking cut that is in one piece.

Combine all the marinade ingredients together. Place the meat in a bowl where it will just fit snugly. Pour the marinade over the meat, cover and marinate for 12 hours, turning 2–3 times.

To cook

Remove the veal from the marinade and wipe with kitchen paper. Pour the oil into a heavy-bottomed casserole. Brown the meat. Turn it on all sides until it is golden. Add the marinade, cover, bring the liquid to the boil and simmer slowly for about 1 hour. Or cook in a 150°C/300°F/gas mark 2 oven for about the same time.

While the meat is cooking

Dissolve the sugar in the vinegar. Be sure all the sugar is dissolved.

To make orange needle shreds

These can be made in advance and kept in a damp piece of kitchen paper in the refrigerator. With a potato peeler carefully peel off pieces of the skin of the oranges, trying not to take any of the white pith. Cut these into needle-thin shreds and blanch in boiling water for 1 minute. Rinse in cold water.

Section the orange

With a serrated fruit knife cut around the skin of the oranges so that there is no pith left. Take the knife and cut between the orange segment and the thin membrane, all round the orange. The segments will come away.

To finish

Stick the point of a knife into the meat to test that it is tender. When the veal is tender, remove and keep warm. In a liquidiser, combine the braising liquid and the stock. Mix for about 5 seconds. The sauce will become a cream colour. Reheat in a small saucepan and whisk in the vinegar. Taste for seasoning.

To serve

Warm the needle shreds and orange sections in the sauce. Carve the veal into thin slices. Place the meat on a warm serving platter, pour some of the sauce and orange sections over the meat and serve the rest in a sauce boat.

LE BOEUF

BEEF

'Beef is the soul of cooking', wrote Antonin Carême, one of the greatest cooks of the nineteenth century. Beef was so important to Louis XVI that when he was caught trying to escape during the Revolution, a supply of short ribs was found in his coach! He wanted to make sure he had something to munch on.

There are many occasions when biting into a rich, succulent piece of beef, served with a suitable red wine, is very satisfying. The sauces I like, allow the natural flavour of the beef to remain dominant, but support and enhance the flavour to provide a memorable meal.

Buying the right cut for your recipe is the first step to success. The best advice I can offer is to get to know your butcher. If you ask questions and show an interest, he will be more interested in serving you and offer you the best choice he has. Look at the meat carefully when you are in a butcher's shop, or for that matter in a supermarket. With a little experience you will quickly get to know what is good and what is better left behind.

Hints on Buying Beef

Lean meat should be bright red when cut. If the beef is old or has been poorly fed it will not brighten after cutting. The fat should be creamy white and firm, not yellow and brittle. Cuts for grilling and roasting should be marbled with fat. This increases tenderness and flavour.

The best cuts for slower cooking usually come from the shoulder area. Remember that even when braising or stewing meat, the better the meat, the better the result. Meat that is fatty will give you a fatty or oily, sauce, resulting in a heavy feeling after your meal.

Cuts of meat very often have different names depending on the area of the country or sometimes on the butcher. Certain butchers specialise in cheaper cuts while others have only the better cuts. I find that knowing the type of meat I need, rather than the specific name, enables me to make the best choice when buying. This way, if a particular cut isn't available or if there is a special price on another cut, I will know what can be substituted to achieve the same result. I have explained the type of meat that is needed in each recipe so that you, too, may get more from your butcher and always have perfect results.

Here is a list of the cuts I have used by type:
FOR GRILLING:
Entrecôte, Fillet, Rumpsteak, Goose skirt, Rump skirt
FOR SLOW COOKING:
Leg of Mutton Cut (This is a whole muscle that is cut off the shoulder and is excellent for slow cooking.)
Chuck or Blade Bone

ENTRECÔTE MARCHAND DU VIN
Steak in Red Wine Sauce

This dish appears on many bistro menus in Paris. It is a delicious traditional recipe and very simple to prepare. The shallots provide the base for the tangy sauce that accentuates the steak.

Cooking time: 15 minutes To serve: 6

INGREDIENTS	METRIC	IMPERIAL	AMERICAN
Entrecôte (sirloin or porterhouse steak) 1 per person each weighing	140–175 g	5–6 oz	5–6 oz
FOR THE SAUCE:			
Shallots, peeled, finely chopped	10	10	10
Butter	50 g	2 oz	¼ cup
Dry red wine	225 ml	8 fl oz	1 cup
Bay leaves	2	2	2
Branch fresh thyme	2	2	2
Crème fraîche	40 ml	3 tbsp	3 tbsp
Cognac	120 ml	4 fl oz	½ cup
Salt and freshly ground black pepper to taste			
TO GARNISH:			
Fresh parsley, chopped	40 g	3 tbsp	3 tbsp

To prepare the sauce
Melt 25 g/1 oz of the butter in a saucepan. Sweat the shallots until transparent. Add the wine, bay leaves, and thyme, raise the heat and reduce the sauce by half. Take out the bay leaves and thyme.

To prepare the steak
In a separate sauté pan, melt 25 g/1 oz of butter and brown the steaks on each side. Salt and pepper the steaks after they are browned. Lower the flame and cook about 2 minutes on each side for rare, or 4–5 minutes for well done. Add the cognac and flambé.

HINT: To flambé, warm the cognac in the pan for a few seconds and then tip the pan so that the gas flame will ignite the liquid. If you have an electric hob throw a lighted match into the warmed cognac. It won't affect the flavour, but before serving remember to remove the match. This method has more purpose than just show. It evaporates the alcohol and caramelises the sugars in it.

Place the steaks on a warmed serving plate and combine the red wine sauce with the juices in the sauté pan. Add the crème fraîche and salt and pepper to taste.

To serve
Pour the sauce over the steak and sprinkle with the chopped parsley. Serve immediately.

Entrecôte Marchand de Vin

BOEUF BRAISÉ
Beef Braised in Red Wine

Braising is a method that can be used to cook many types of food. The food is first browned and then cooked in a tightly covered casserole with very little liquid. In this case the meat is made tender by marinating it overnight. It then cooks very slowly, absorbing all the flavours of its braising liquid.

Cooking time: 2½–3 hours To serve: 6–8

INGREDIENTS	METRIC	IMPERIAL	AMERICAN
FOR THE MARINADE:			
Onion, sliced	1 med	1 med	1 med
Carrot, sliced	1	1	1
Garlic, crushed	1 clove	1 clove	1 clove
Olive oil	15 ml	1 tbsp	1 tbsp
Red wine (A fuller bodied wine such as Maçon, is desirable)	350 ml	12 fl oz	1½ cups
TO BRAISE:			
Leg of mutton cut of beef, or any braising beef in 1 piece	1.4 kg	3 lbs	3 lbs
Oil	40 ml	3 tbsp	3 tbsp
Onion, sliced	1 large	1 large	1 large
Carrots, sliced	2	2	2
Garlic, crushed	1 clove	1 clove	1 clove
Brown stock	150 ml	5 fl oz	⅔ cup
Red wine	175 ml	6 fl oz	¾ cup
Bouquet garni (few stalks of parsley, 2 branches fresh thyme, 1 bay leaf tied together)			
Salt and pepper to taste			
Button mushrooms, sliced	175 g	6 oz	1½ cups
TO GARNISH:			
Glazed button onions or pickling onions and glazed carrots (page 99)			

HINT: If using stock cubes, use half chicken and half beef.

To make the marinade
Combine all the ingredients in a saucepan and bring to the boil. Boil for about 2 minutes and cool. Place the meat in a bowl that just fits it snugly. Pour the marinade over it and be sure the meat is covered. Leave in the refrigerator for about 12 hours or longer. Turn from time to time.

To braise the meat
Wipe the meat dry with kitchen paper. Save the marinade.

Heat the oil in a heavy-bottomed casserole and brown the meat on all sides. Keep moving the meat to keep it from sticking. Remove the meat and put in the onion and carrots. Sauté until they start to shrivel and turn colour slightly.

Return the meat to the casserole and add the garlic, stock, wine and bouquet garni. Add a little salt and pepper. Cover and bring to the boil. Lower the heat and simmer gently for 2½–3 hours. Or, after bringing the liquid to the boil, place in an oven at 150°C/300°F/gas mark 2 for the same time, covering it with a piece of grease-proof paper and a lid. Turn the meat occasionally. Add the mushrooms to the meat about 20 minutes before the end.

While the meat is cooking, glaze the onions and carrots (page 99).

To prepare the sauce
When the meat is tender, take it out, skim all of the fat off the cooking liquid and strain. Reduce the liquid by half.

Liquidise the marinade with the vegetables. Add the reduced braising juices to the liquidised marinade. Strain the mixture, making sure to press firmly on all of the vegetables to extract their juice. The pulp that seeps through the sieve will be enough to thicken the sauce. Warm the sauce and taste for seasoning, adding more salt

and pepper if necessary.
To serve
Thinly slice the meat and arrange on a warm serving dish. Heat the sauce through and add the glazed onions and carrots. Pour over the meat and serve.

OIGNONS DORÉS
Glazed Onions

INGREDIENTS	METRIC	IMPERIAL	AMERICAN
Small button or pickling onions	225 g	8 oz	½ lb
Sugar	5 g	1 tsp	1 tsp
Butter	15 g	½ oz	1 tbsp
Salt and pepper to taste			

Peel the onions.

> *HINT: The easiest way is to blanch the onions first. Bring water to the boil add the onions and wait for the water to return to the boil. Drain and plunge into cold water. The skins will then come off easily.*

Place them in a pot with water to cover. Bring the water to the boil and cook the onions until they are tender, about 10–15 minutes. Prick with a knife to test to see if the onions are soft all the way through. Drain and return to the pan. Add the sugar, butter, salt and pepper. Cover and cook over low heat for about 10 minutes, shaking the pan now and then. The onions should be coated with a sticky brown glaze.

CAROTTES GLACÉS
Glazed Carrots

INGREDIENTS	METRIC	IMPERIAL	AMERICAN
Carrots	680 g	1½ lb	1½ lb
Chicken stock	425 g	15 fl oz	2 cups
Sugar	25 g	2 tbsp	2 tbsp
Butter	75 g	3 oz	⅓ cup
Salt and freshly ground black pepper			

Peel the carrots and cut them to the size of a small, new or baby carrot, about 35 mm/1½ in by 12 mm/½ in. Place all of the ingredients in a saucepan and bring to a slow boil, uncovered. Boil for about 30 to 40 minutes until nearly all of the liquid has reduced and the carrots are coated with a syrupy glaze. Shake the pan as the liquid reduces to keep the carrots from sticking.

GOULASH À LA HONGROISE
Hungarian Goulash

A Frenchman will tell you that his cuisine is the best in the world and that all of the world's best recipes originate in France. I am not sure whether *Goulash à la Hongroise* originated in France or whether it has been adapted because of its fine qualities.

The secret of this light and colourful dish is the type of paprika used. It should be true Hungarian paprika, freshly bought. This recipe can be made ahead and freezes well.

Cooking time: 2 hours To serve: 6

INGREDIENTS	METRIC	IMPERIAL	AMERICAN
Braising beef, or any slow cooking cut such as leg of mutton cut, cut into 5 cm/2 in cubes	900 g	2 lbs	2 lbs
Oil	25 ml	2 tbsp	2 tbsp
Onions, chopped	2 large	2 large	2 large
Hungarian paprika	40 g	3 tbsp	3 tbsp
Flour	15 g	1 tbsp	1 tbsp
Chicken stock	450 ml	16 fl oz	2 cups
Tomato purée (paste)	15 ml	1 tbsp	1 tbsp
Bouquet garni (a few parsley stalks, branch fresh thyme, 1 bay leaf tied together)			
Clove garlic, crushed	1	1	1
Salt and freshly ground black pepper to taste			
TO GARNISH:			
Sweet pimentos, canned	185 g	6.5 oz	¾ cup
Tomatoes	2 large	2 large	2 large
Crème fraîche	25–40 ml	2–3 tbsp	2–3 tbsp

HINT: If you cut up your meat in very small cubes, it will cook to nothing.

Carefully brown the meat in the oil.

HINT: Each time you put a piece of meat in the pan it lowers the temperature. Thus, if you put all of the meat in at once, you will find the meat steaming instead of browning. To avoid this place 1 or 2 pieces in at a time. When the fat is sizzling again add another piece, thus giving the pan a chance to regain the high temperature needed. Take out the pieces as they brown.

HINT: When sautéing any meat, move it around the pan as soon as it is put in. This stops it sticking. If your meat does stick, then that area will burn and ruin your sauce later on.

When all the meat is browned, take it out and sweat the onions until transparent. Add the paprika. Let the mixture cook for a few minutes to release the flavour of the paprika. Add the flour and cook for another minute. Add the meat and then the stock. The stock should nearly cover the meat. Add the tomato purée and bouquet garni. Stir to make sure all the ingredients are blended. Add the garlic and a little salt and pepper.

Cover and simmer slowly for 1½–2 hours until the meat is tender. (If you want to cook it in the oven, bring the liquid to the boil, place a piece of greaseproof paper over the meat to keep it moist, cover and place in the oven at 170°C/325°F/gas mark 3 for the same time.) Take out the bouquet garni. Add salt and pepper to taste. The goulash can be cooled and frozen at this point. If you do this, defrost and re-warm slowly.

To garnish

Slice the pimento in thin strips. Skin, quarter and de-seed the tomatoes.

HINT: To peel the tomatoes, blanch by placing in boiling water for 8–12 seconds and plunge into cold water. Then peel.

Goulash à la Hongroise

To serve
Place the goulash on a warmed serving platter. Place the crème fraîche in spoonfuls around the platter. Don't mix it in. It looks quite pretty with the white cream showing and the pimentos and tomatoes scattered around for colour. The cream will mix in as it is served.

101

BOEUF STROGANOFF
Beef Stroganoff

The Russian influence in French cuisine was important long before the Russian Revolution sent the nobility scurrying to Paris for refuge. One of my favourite spots for lunch in Paris was the Conservatory of Music where a charming old Russian couple served the most delicious examples of Russian food. This stroganoff is a mixture of Russian flavour and French ingenuity.

Cooking time: 20 minutes To serve: 6

INGREDIENTS	METRIC	IMPERIAL	AMERICAN
Rumpsteak or goose skirt	680–900 g	1½–2 lbs	1½–2 lbs
Butter	50 g	2 oz	¼ cup
Onions, chopped	3 large	3 large	3 large
Mushrooms, sliced	275 g	10 oz	2½ cups
Flour	18 g	1½ tbsp	1½ tbsp
Brown stock	400 ml	14 fl oz	1¾ cups
Tomato purée (paste)	175 g	6 oz	¾ cup
Several drops of Worcestershire sauce			
Pinch of sugar			
Mustard	10 ml	2 tsp	2 tsp
Salt and freshly ground black pepper to taste			
Crème fraîche	85 ml	6 tbsp	6 tbsp
TO GARNISH:			
Fresh parsley, chopped	25 g	2 tbsp	2 tbsp

HINT: (680 g/1½ lbs of steak is quite sufficient for 6 people when served as part of a three course meal. However, if you like a large main course only, use 2 lbs.)

Slice the meat in thin strips about ½ cm/¼ in thick. (If using goose skirt, slice against the grain.) Place the butter in a heavy-bottomed pan and sauté a few pieces at a time. Try not to overcook them. The meat should be juicy and slightly rare. As soon as they are browned take them out of the pan.

Add the onions and sweat them until they are transparent. (Sauté them for a few minutes and then add a few drops of water, cover with a piece of greaseproof paper and a lid. Let them sweat in this way until they look clear). Add the mushrooms and cook for a few minutes. Add the flour, and cook for one minute. Pour in the stock. Add the tomato purée, Worcestershire sauce, sugar, mustard, and salt and pepper to taste. You may need to add a little more of the Worcestershire sauce or sugar according to your taste.

HINT: The recipe can be made a few hours in advance to this point.

Just before serving add the cream, and again taste for seasoning. Add the meat to the warm sauce and gently let it warm through, being careful not to overcook the meat.

To serve
Place on a warmed serving platter and sprinkle chopped parsley on top for colour.

STEAK AU POIVRE
Steak with Pepper Sauce

This very simple and very French dish is always a success and, best of all, takes only a few minutes to make. The traditional method is to serve a small steak per person. However, if you have several people, you may grill one large steak and make the sauce separately.

Cooking time: approximately 15 min To serve: 4

INGREDIENTS	METRIC	IMPERIAL	AMERICAN
Porterhouse steak, 1 per person	140–175 g each	5–6 oz each	5–6 oz each
Poivre steak (These are broken white or black peppercorns and can be bought ready prepared in the spice section of most shops)		approx. 1 tbs for each steak	
Butter	70 g	2½ oz	½ cup + 1 tbsp
Flour	40 g	1½ oz	⅓ cup
Beef stock	250 ml	9 fl oz	1 cup + 2 tbsp
Cognac	25 ml	2 tbsp	2 tbsp
Crème fraîche	25 ml	2 tbsp	2 tbsp

HINT: Any tender grilling steak will do: rump, fillet steak, goose skirt.

HINT: If using stock cubes, use half beef stock and half chicken stock.

To prepare steak
Cover the steak with the poivre steak and press it into the meat with the palm of your hand. Melt the butter in a heavy-bottomed sauté pan. Raise the heat and brown the steaks on each side, lower the heat and cook until done. For rare meat about 3 minutes on each side is sufficient. For well done about 5 minutes on each side. Try not to overcook or the meat will be dry and flavourless. Remove the steak to a warm serving dish and cover to keep warm.

To prepare the sauce
Add the flour to the sauté pan and let cook slowly over a low heat in the juices and fat until it becomes a deep russet colour. This is called a roux brun. If it seems too dry add more butter. Add the beef stock and raise the heat to reduce the liquid by about half. Add the cognac and cook for 1 minute. Add the crème fraîche. Taste for salt and pepper.

To serve
Pour the sauce over the steak and serve immediately.

STEAK FARCI
Stuffed Barbecued Steak

For those people who love to barbecue, this recipe will offer a pleasant change and will help your steak go further. It can also be grilled inside, if you prefer, and will produce a good result.

Cooking Time: 20 mins for farce and steak
To serve: 6

INGREDIENTS	METRIC	IMPERIAL	AMERICAN
Rump steak or rump skirt (thick middle section)	680–900 g	1½–2 lbs	1½–2 lbs
FOR THE SAUCE:			
Shallot, finely chopped (10 g/2 tsp onion may be used)	1	1	1
Butter	25 g	1 oz	2 tbs
Mushrooms, finely chopped	100 g	4 oz	1 cup
Salt and freshly ground black pepper to taste			
Ham, chopped	15 g	1 tbsp	1 tbsp
Fresh parsley, chopped	5 g	1 tsp	1 tsp
Fresh thyme, chopped	5 g	1 tsp	1 tsp
Bread crumbs	15 g	1 tbsp	1 tbsp

HINT: The steak should be (1½–2 in/4 cm–5 cm) thick so that a slit can be made.

To prepare farce
Sweat the chopped shallot in the butter until transparent. Add the chopped mushrooms and salt and pepper. Cook until the liquid has evaporated. Add the ham, parsley, thyme and bread crumbs. Taste for seasoning. Cool.

To prepare steak
Slit the steak in half lengthwise, and salt and pepper the inside of the steak.

HINT: Ask the butcher to slit the steak for you. It will only take him a minute.

Fill the slit with the stuffing. Sew the steak closed with string. Brush the outside with oil and place on a hot barbecue or grill for 4–5 mins on each side for rare. Cook it longer if you want it well done.

HINT: If you wish to stuff the meat a few hours before cooking, be sure the stuffing is cold and keep it in the refrigerator after it is stuffed. Take out about 20 mins before cooking.

To serve
Carve and serve immediately.

Steak Farci

L'AGNEAU
LAMB

Mrs. Beeton famous for her Book on Household Management once wrote that lamb is: 'of all wild or domesticated animals ... without exception, the most useful to man as food.' This is particularly true throughout the Middle East and China where lamb forms the basis of their meat diet. Throughout French history lamb has gone in and out of favour. The classic gigot d'agneau *(leg of lamb) is still much loved as is* carré d'agneau *(rack of lamb). The French like their lamb young or, as the British call it, spring lamb, and rare. They consider it at its best when juicy and pink.*

Lamb is a very special meat in Britain. In fact, English ranchers tried to introduce it to the western United States. However, beef won the battle. What a loss for the colonials. Good British lamb with its subtle flavour makes a superb dinner party dish.

Here are some hints about buying lamb:
Modern methods of raising lamb mean that we can have lamb chops all year round. However, the lamb season really starts in April when *agneau de lait* or lamb that is 2–3 months old and raised on milk becomes readily available. After this period we have spring lamb which is 3–4 months old. As the season progresses, lamb gets heavier and in the winter time a leg of lamb can weigh over 6 lbs. With the modern emphasis on light cooking I prefer to use young and tender lamb which has a more delicate taste and is less fatty.

AGNEAU PROVENÇAL
Lamb with the Flavour of Provence

When I first encountered this dish, I was astounded to learn that there were 4 whole heads of garlic as an integral part of it. Luckily, I found this out *after* having tasted its delicious flavour, which was not at all overpowered by garlic. In fact, what one does taste are the flavoursome Herbes de Provence. These can be bought in most delicatessens. However, they are quite easy to prepare and will have a fresher quality if mixed at home.

Cooking time: 1½–1¾ hours To serve: 6

INGREDIENTS	METRIC	IMPERIAL	AMERICAN
Olive oil	40 ml	3 tbs	3 tbs
Shoulder of lamb, boned and cut into 5 cm/2 in cubes	1.4 kg	3 lbs	3 lbs
Dry white wine	225 ml	8 fl oz	1 cup
Heads of garlic, unpeeled	4	4	4
Chicken stock	450 ml	16 fl oz	2 cups
Large bouquet garni (several stalks of parsley, 4 branches fresh thyme, 1 bay leaf)			
Herbes de Provence	25 g	2–3 tbsp	2–3 tbsp
Salt and freshly ground black pepper to taste			
FOR THE GARNISH:			
Chopped parsley			

HINT: If using a good quality olive oil, mix half and half with corn oil. Many of the cheaper olive oils in the market have already been mixed with a vegetable oil.

Heat the oil in a heavy-bottomed casserole and add the meat a few pieces at a time. Move each piece as it touches the oil to keep it from sticking. As the fat re-gains its heat, add more cubes of meat. When each piece is browned, remove from the pan. Continue in this way until all the meat is browned. Remove the meat and pour off the fat. Pour in about 50 ml/2 fl oz of the white wine and deglaze the pan: scrape the brown parts from the bottom and mix into the wine.

HINT: If the bottom of your pan has turned black while browning the meat, wash out the pan before adding the wine. The burned parts will ruin your sauce.

Place the meat back in the pan. With the flat part of a large knife, firmly tap the garlic heads so that the individual cloves will fall away. Bruise the cloves by tapping again to release some of the juices. Put into the casserole with the meat. Add the bouquet garni and sprinkle in the Herbes de Provence.

HINT: Either tie the herbs together with kitchen string or wrap them in some butter muslin (cheese cloth).

Pour over the rest of the wine. Bring to a simmer to cook off the alcohol. Add the stock and cover with a piece of greaseproof paper and a lid. Simmer gently on a hob for 1½–1¾ hours, or bring the liquid to a boil and place in an oven at 180°C/350°F/gas mark 4 for the same time. Test the meat. It should feel soft when pierced by a knife.

To make the sauce
Remove the meat with a slotted spoon and remove the garlic. Purée the garlic through a sieve or in a food mill. Take all the fat off the sauce and reduce to about 425 ml/15 fl oz/2 cups. Add the puréed garlic and taste. Add salt and pepper.

To serve
Place the meat on a warm serving platter and pour the sauce over it. Sprinkle with chopped parsley for colour.

To prepare the recipe in advance
Cook the meat for about 1½ hours. Turn off and let the meat cool in the liquid. Store in the refrigerator. Bring to room temperature before re-heating. Make the sauce as above.

To make herbes de Provence
Use fresh herbs that you have dried yourself, or buy herbs that are on their branches and have been properly dried. Take the leaves off the branches and blend them together in a food processor or blender in the following proportions:

1 measure marjoram
1 measure oregano
2 measures thyme
1 measure saurriette or summer savory

NOISETTES D'AGNEAU
Lamb Noisettes

A noisette literally means little nut. In fact, it is a boned lamb cutlet. This dish is best in the spring when you can have the very finest of milk-fed lamb. The delicate flavour of the young lamb is brought out in this recipe. Ask the butcher to bone, roll, and cut the noisettes for you. The rest of the dish takes very little time.

Cooking time: approximately 15 minutes To serve: 6

INGREDIENTS	METRIC	IMPERIAL	AMERICAN
Best end neck of lamb made into noisettes	12	12	12
Oil	15 ml	1 tbsp	1 tbsp
FOR SAUCE:			
Sherry	175 ml	6 fl oz	¾ cup
Chicken stock	175 ml	6 fl oz	¾ cup
FOR SALPICON:			
Onion, chopped	1 small	1 small	1 small
Cucumbers, cut into julienne strips	2	2	2
Butter	25 g	1 oz	2 tbsp
Fresh mint, chopped	15 g	1 tbsp	1 tbsp
Double (heavy) cream	25 ml	2 tbsp	2 tbsp

HINT: It is very simple to make the noisettes yourself. All you need is a very sharp, small knife. Cut along the bones with the knife held firmly against the bone using short even strokes. Lift out each bone as it is freed. Roll and tie the lamb and cut into noisettes.

To make the salpicon
Sweat the onions until transparent. Blanch the cucumbers: bring a pan of water to the boil and put the cucumbers in; as soon as the water comes back to the boil, drain and refresh in cold water. Add the cucumbers to the onions. They should still be a little firm. Add the mint. Shake the pan over the heat or gently toss the ingredients simply to warm through. Try not to stir with a spoon and break up the julienne strips. Add the cream. Taste for seasoning. Add salt and pepper as needed. This salpicon can be made in advance and gently re-warmed. If you do this, add the mint during the re-warming.

To cook the noisettes
Heat the oil in a frying pan and place one noisette in at a time, moving it as soon as it touches the pan to prevent it sticking. As soon as the fat is sizzling again, add another. Brown the meat on each side to seal. Salt and pepper the cooked side. Continue in this way until all of the noisettes have been sealed. The lamb should cook about 1–2 minutes on each side. Remove from the pan, pour off the excess fat, and deglaze the pan with the sherry, scraping off all of the brown bits from the pan and mixing in the sherry. Add the stock and raise the heat to reduce by a third. The recipe may be prepared ahead to this point up to an hour before serving. Do not refrigerate. Place the lamb in an ovenproof serving dish.

To finish
Place the noisettes under the grill to finish cooking them through. This should take about 5 minutes. The lamb should be pink when served. Place the lamb in a circle on a warmed serving platter (if you have not used an ovenproof platter earlier). If your grill is not large enough, the noisettes can be finished in the oven. Warm the sherry sauce and the salpicon. Spoon the sherry sauce over the grilled noisettes and spoon the salpicon in a row down the centre of the platter.

To serve
For each person serve 2 noisettes and a little salpicon on the side.

Noisettes d'Agneau

AGNEAU FARCI AU CITRON

Stuffed Lamb in Lemon Sauce

The blend of lemon with the lamb in this recipe gives it a refreshing flavour. The stuffing can be made in advance, but the lamb should be stuffed and roasted just before serving. If one is serving a large dinner party, the lamb can be undercooked and carved a few hours before the guests are to arrive. The sauce can then be finished and the dish assembled and gently re-warmed just before serving.

Cooking time: 40–50 minutes To serve: 6

INGREDIENTS	METRIC	IMPERIAL	AMERICAN
Loin or best end neck of lamb, boned (the butcher will do this)	1.4 kg	3 lbs	3 lbs
Salt and freshly ground pepper to taste			
FOR THE STUFFING:			
Butter	25 g	1 oz	2 tbsp
Onion, chopped	1 med	1 med	1 med
Dry bread crumbs	140 g	5 oz	½ cup + 1 tbsp
Fresh sage, chopped	25 g	2 tbsp	2 tbsp
Fresh parsley, chopped	25 g	2 tbsp	2 tbsp
Fresh thyme, chopped (If using dried herbs, use half the amount. They will be stronger.)	25 g	2 tbsp	2 tbsp
Lemon, zest and juice	½	½	½
Egg	1	1	1
FOR SAUCE:			
Onion, sliced	1 large	1 large	1 large
Flour	15 g	1 tbsp	1 tbsp
Chicken stock	300 ml	10 fl oz	1¼ cups
Redcurrant jelly	40 ml	3 tbsp	3 tbsp
Lemon, juice	½	½	½

Pre-heat the oven to 200°C/400°F/gas mark 6. Open the boned lamb and lie it flat in front of you. Salt and pepper the inside of the meat.

To make the stuffing

Melt the butter in a small frying pan and sweat the onion until transparent. Mix the onions into the bread crumbs. Add the fresh herbs, zest of lemon, and salt and pepper. Bind the mixture together with some of the lemon juice. Taste for seasoning. Add more salt and pepper if necessary. The stuffing should be well seasoned. Lightly beat the egg and mix it into the stuffing.

To roast the meat

Cut as much of the fat off the lamb as possible. Place the stuffing evenly over the meat. Roll the lamb together and tie around with kitchen string at about 55 mm/2 in intervals.

Place in a roasting tin and put in the oven for about 40 minutes. The lamb should be pink when finished. Take out and place on a warm platter with some foil over it to keep warm. Leave it in a warm spot near the oven.

To make the sauce

Tip all the fat out of the roasting tin. Place the tin on a hob and add the sliced onion. Sauté slowly until it is browned. Add the flour and cook for 1 minute. Add the stock and let the sauce reduce in the tin. Cream the jelly by mixing it well, so that there are no lumps and add to the sauce. Add the juice of half a lemon, salt and pepper. Taste. Add more lemon juice or jelly as needed. It should not be too sweet.

To serve

Slice the lamb and remove the string. Place on serving platter with a little of the sauce over it. Serve the rest of the sauce in a sauce boat.

If you are preparing this recipe several hours in advance, undercook the lamb, set it aside and make the sauce. Slice the lamb when ready to serve, add a little more sauce to the serving platter and cover with foil. Gently rewarm in the oven for about 15 minutes and serve. Make sure that you do not overcook the lamb.

LE PORC

PORK

In his writings the eighteenth century food enthusiast Grimond de la Reyniere said the pig is 'a veritable walking repast. One throws no part of it away, even to the feet, one eats it all.' There is no waste on the pig, not only because almost all of it can be eaten, but because those parts that cannot are still useful, the skin for leather, the stomach for pepsin, the hair for upholstery and insulation. For our purposes the meat is quite versatile and lends itself to inexpensive meals that can also be very elegant.

Pork, very often, is relegated to family meals and not considered good enough for guests or special evenings. Today, the farming of pork is so sophisticated that it produces an excellent meat that is not fatty or overpowering. My local butcher's pork is so light in colour that many people think it is veal at first glance. My dinner guests have thoroughly enjoyed the pork recipes I have included.

Here are some hints about buying and cooking pork:

There has always been a fear about underdone pork. We have all been told that pork must be well cooked to kill the trichinae in it. It was well established in 1919, that trichinae are killed when the meat reaches a temperature of 60°C/137°F. Since pork is still quite juicy and tender when the meat thermometer reaches 80°C/180°F, there is really no reason to cook it to a higher temperature until it is dry and tough.

When buying pork either from a butcher or supermarket, I always ask if it has been frozen. For some reason many of the cuts of pork are frozen when delivered to the shop and thawed before selling to the customer. This seems to be particularly true of pork fillets. There is nothing wrong with this method of distribution. However, if it has been frozen, it should be eaten right away and not refrozen.

Here are some hints about the cuts I have used:

Loin of pork: This cut is usually boned and can be stuffed and rolled. When I have it boned, I ask for the bones to add to my sauce for texture and flavour. When bought from a good supplier, this cut looks almost white.

Fillet or tenderloin: This is the finest cut of pork. It corresponds to the fillet of beef and has very little fat. It must be carefully cooked or it will be dry.

Pork chops: These are sold with or without the kidney section which tends to have a stronger flavour. This depends on which section of the ribs the chop comes from. You can ask for either.

FILET DE PORC FARCI
Stuffed Pork Fillets

This dish uses pork fillets which are split in half lengthwise and stuffed. The apple, walnut and raisin stuffing complements the pork beautifully. To add a finishing touch to this marriage, it is served with a sauce made with apple cider. The stuffing can also be used for veal or poultry.

Cooking time: 40 minutes To serve: 6–8

INGREDIENTS	METRIC	IMPERIAL	AMERICAN
4 pork fillets, all about the same length, each weighing about	340 g	12 oz	12 oz
Salt and freshly ground pepper to taste			
Oil to brush the fillets, about	50 ml	2 oz	¼ cup
Rosemary, thyme and oregano, approximately	25 g	2 tbsp	2 tbsp
FOR STUFFING:			
Butter	25g	1 oz	2 tbsp
Shallot, finely chopped (15 g/1 tbsp chopped onion may be substituted)	1	1	1
Walnuts, chopped	40 g	1½ oz	1½ oz
Raisins, washed, chopped	50 g	2 oz	½ cup
Apple, chopped	1	1	1
Bread crumbs	50 g	2 oz	¼ cup
Fresh parsley, chopped	15 g	1 tbsp	1 tbsp
Egg	1	1	1
FOR THE SAUCE:			
Cider	600 ml	1 pt	2½ cups
Crème fraîche	85 ml	6 tbsp	6 tbsp

Pre-heat oven to 200°C/400°F/gas mark 6.
With a sharp knife slit the fillets lengthwise. Open them flat and bat out. If you don't have a meat bat use the bottom of a frying pan, the end of a milk bottle, or the end of a rolling pin to flatten the meat. Salt and pepper the inside.

To make the stuffing
Sauté the shallot in the butter for 5 minutes until transparent. Remove from the heat. Mix with the walnuts, raisins, apple, bread crumbs and parsley. Add salt and pepper and taste for seasoning. Add more salt and pepper if necessary. Mix in the egg.

To fill the fillets
Lay the stuffing down the centre of 2 of the fillets. Take the other fillets and place over the top of the stuffed ones, to make two cylindrical shapes. Tie string round the fillets at approximately 5 cm/2 in intervals. Brush the fillets with a little oil and sprinkle with some fresh herbs such as thyme, rosemary, oregano or any combination of these herbs.

To roast
Place the fillets in a roasting pan and roast in the oven for 40 minutes. Try not to overcook them.

To make the sauce
Place the fillets on a carving board and cover with some foil to keep them warm. Deglaze the roasting tin with the cider: place the roasting tin on a hob and gently heat while pouring in the cider; scrape all of the coagulated brown bits into the sauce. Raise the heat and reduce the liquid to about half. Add salt and pepper and taste. Add more if necessary. Add crème fraîche and mix well.

To serve
Remove the string. Thinly slice the pork and arrange in layers in a warmed serving platter. Pour a little sauce over the meat and serve the rest in a sauce boat.

To make this dish in advance, slice the meat and place on an ovenproof serving dish. Pour a little sauce over the meat to keep it moist. Cover with foil. When ready to serve, re-warm it in a low oven for about 15 minutes. I suggest that the meat be kept no more than a few hours before serving. Do not refrigerate it.

*34 Filet de Porc Farci avec Broccoli aux Graines de
Sésame (p 118)*

113

RÔTI DE PORC FARCI AU CALVADOS

Stuffed Loin of Pork with Calvados Sauce

Cooking time: 1½ hours To serve: 6–8

INGREDIENTS	METRIC	IMPERIAL	AMERICAN
Loin of pork, wing end, boned (not rolled) (reserve the bones for the sauce)	1.1 kg	2½ lb	2½ lb
Butter	25 g	1 oz	2 tbsp
Oil	15 ml	1 tbsp	1 tbsp
Calvados	15 ml	1 tbsp	1 tbsp
FOR FARCE:			
Mushrooms, chopped	100 g	4 oz	1 cup
Butter	25 g	1 oz	12 tbsp
Fresh sage, chopped (if dried sage is used, use half the amount)	25 g	2 tbsp	2 tbsp
Calvados	40 ml	3 tbsp	3 tbsp
Sausage meat	175 g	6 oz	6 oz
FOR SAUCE:			
Water or chicken stock	50 ml	2 fl oz	¼ cup
Calvados	25 ml	2 tbsp	2 tbsp
Crème fraîche	25 ml	2 tbsp	2 tbsp
Salt and freshly ground pepper to taste			

Lay the pork out flat on a board. With a sharp knife cut lengthwise through the thick part of the meat. Open it flat. Salt and pepper the inside of the meat.

To make the farce
Sauté the mushrooms in the butter until all of the juices have evaporated (about 3 minutes). Mix the mushrooms, calvados, sage, salt and pepper into the sausage meat. Take a small pinch of the farce and fry it to taste for seasoning.

HINT: When making any kind of stuffing, be sure to season it well. Stuffing seems to absorb seasoning and should always be tasted while making to avoid it being bland.

Place on the meat, roll up and tie.

HINT: Be careful not to overfill the meat. The stuffing will expand and spill into the pan. It will then burn and ruin your sauce.

Tie at about 5 cm/2 in intervals to hold the meat firmly in place. Melt the butter and oil in a casserole that is just big enough to fit the meat snugly.

HINT: If the casserole is too big, the juices will run over the bottom and evaporate.

Brown the meat on all sides. Add half of the calvados and flambé.

HINT: To flambé, warm the calvados in the pan for a few seconds and then tip the pan so that the gas flame will ignite the liquid. If you have an electric hob, throw a lighted match into the warmed calvados. It won't affect the flavour, but before serving remember to remove the match. This method has more purpose that just show. It evaporates the alcohol and caramelises the sugars in it.

Add the bones and cover. Simmer over low heat for 1 hour and 15 minutes, turning the meat a couple of times. Remove from the casserole and cover with foil to keep warm.

To make sauce
Skim all of the fat off the sauce and add the crème fraîche and the remaining calvados. Taste and add salt and pepper as needed.

To serve
Thinly slice the pork and arrange on a warm serving platter. Pour some of the sauce over it and serve the rest in a sauce boat. If serving cold, omit the sauce. If preparing in advance, leave the meat whole in the casserole. Gently warm it, slice, and make the sauce.

CÔTES DE PORC AU WHISKY

Pork Chops in Whisky Sauce

This is a very quick recipe with a delicious and unusual sauce. I find that boneless pork chops which are very popular now are excellent for this method of cooking. Veal or chicken can be substituted for the pork.

Cooking time: 10 minutes To serve: 6

INGREDIENTS	METRIC	IMPERIAL	AMERICAN
Butter	25 g	1 oz	2 tbsp
Oil	15 ml	1 tbsp	1 tbsp
One pork chop per person	6	6	6
Salt and freshly ground black pepper to taste			
Whisky	175 ml	6 fl oz	¾ cup
Beef stock	200 ml	7 fl oz	scant cup
Brown sugar	40 g	1½ oz	⅓ cup
Dijon mustard	15 g	1 tbsp	1 tbsp
Potato flour or arrowroot	5 g	1 tsp	1 tsp
Cold water	25 ml	1 fl oz	1 oz

To brown the meat

Melt the butter and oil in a heavy-bottomed sauté or frying pan. When the fat is hot, put in one chop and move it as soon as it touches the pan. As it browns, turn it and salt and pepper the cooked side. When the fat is hot again add the next chop. Continue in this way until all of the chops are browned. Pour off any excess fat. Add the whisky and flambé.

HINT: To flambé, warm the whisky in the pan for a few seconds and then tip the pan so that the gas flame will ignite the liquid. If you have an electric hob, throw a lighted match into the warmed whisky. It won't affect the flavour, but before serving remember to remove the match. This method has more purpose than just show. It evaporates the alcohol and caramelises the sugars in it.

To cook the meat

Add the stock, then the sugar and mustard. Blend well together. Cover the pan and lower the heat. Cook at a low simmer for 5 minutes or until the chops are cooked. This will, obviously depend on the size of the chops. Try not to overcook them or they will be dry.

To finish the sauce

Take out the chops and place on a warmed serving platter. Cover with foil to keep warm. Put the potato flour and water in a small glass and mix well. Pour into the sauce and cook until it thickens. This will take about 1 minute. Add salt and pepper to taste.

To serve

Pour some of the sauce over the chops and serve the rest in a sauce boat. Serve immediately.

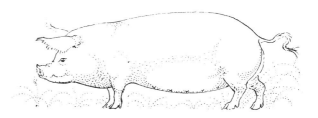

CÔTES DE PORC BONNE FEMME

Pork Chops Bonne Femme

The sauce for this recipe is made separately and can be made in advance. It goes perfectly with pork chops, but is also excellent with other cuts of pork, chicken, or veal.

Cooking time: 20 minutes for sauce and meat To serve: 6

INGREDIENTS	METRIC	IMPERIAL	AMERICAN
Butter	25 g	1 oz	2 tbsp
Pork chops, 1 per person, or 2 if small			
FOR SAUCE:			
Onions, sliced	3 large	3 large	3 large
Butter	25 g	1 oz	2 tbsp
Small tomatoes, quartered	12	12	12
Dry red wine	225 ml	8 fl oz	1 cup
Crème fraîche	150 ml	5 fl oz	2/3 cup
Salt and freshly ground black pepper to taste			
TO GARNISH:			
Chopped parsley	25 g	2 tbsp	2 tbsp

HINT: If tomatoes are out of season, use tinned ones. They will be of better quality. Two 200 g/8 oz tins will do.

To make the sauce

Sweat the onions in the butter until they are transparent. Add the tomatoes and wine. Cover and let simmer until the tomatoes have cooked to a sauce. Add salt and pepper and taste for seasoning.

HINT: If the sauce looks a bit watery, remove the lid and let it reduce until it is the consistency of thick cream. The thickness of the sauce will depend on the type of tomatoes, some are juicier than others.

To cook the pork

Melt the butter in a large frying pan. Brown one pork chop over a high heat. Turn it over and salt and pepper the browned side. Add another chop to the pan as soon as the fat is sizzling again. Always salt and pepper the cooked side. Continue in this way until all of the chops are browned. Lower the flame and let the chops cook through. This should take 5–10 minutes depending on the size of the chops.

To serve

Warm the sauce and add the crème fraîche and taste for salt and pepper. Pour the sauce onto a serving platter and then lay the chops on the sauce. Sprinkle with chopped parsley for colour. Serve.

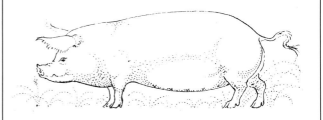

LES LÉGUMES
VEGETABLES

Light, colourful, and full of flavour, vegetables play an important role in completing a dinner menu. Not only are they an important food source, but they also provide pleasing visual and taste effects. In France very often the first course is a hot or cold vegetable. Beautifully cooked asparagus or a colourful display of different vegetable purées, perhaps served in pastry appear interesting and are fun to taste. I have selected a cross section of vegetable recipes to show the various methods of cooking vegetables, and to widen your choice of presentation.

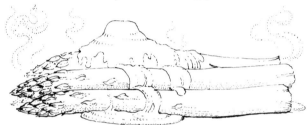

General rules for cooking vegetables
A vegetable that grows above the ground should, in general, be cooked in boiling water without a lid.
A root vegetable should be placed in cold water, covered and then cooked.

Either way it is important not to overcook vegetables. The French blanch their green vegetables. They put them in a pot of boiling water. When the water comes back to the boil, they are drained and refreshed in cold water. This will set the colour, and stop the cooking to keep the vegetables green and crisp. They are then either re-heated in hot water for a few minutes or tossed in a frying pan with butter to warm through.

Some hints on selecting vegetables
Try to choose your vegetables carefully. They should look like a beautiful picture: shiny, full of colour and firm. However, I'm not always successful in my search for top quality produce. If I consistently receive mediocre vegetables from my greengrocer, I take them back or mention it the next time I see him. If we demand quality food, then we will improve our chance of getting it.

Try to pick vegetables that are in season. We can now buy a greater variety of vegetables from all over the world. With quick air travel, many of these reach us at their peak. However, nothing can match the flavour of vegetables that are grown close by and rushed to market the day after they are picked. It's always amusing to listen to the market men squabbling over the claim to the best asparagus. Whether it is French, Belgian, or Californian, the best tasting produce has the shortest time between picking and eating.

Vegetables can be the high point of your meal. Recognise their benefit as a lighter food with less fat and calories.

JULIENNE DE COURGETTES ET DE CAROTTES

Courgette and Carrot Matchsticks

The colourful matchstick vegetables are light and tasty and go well with any type of meat or fish.

Cooking time: 10–15 minutes To serve: 6

INGREDIENTS	METRIC	IMPERIAL	AMERICAN
Carrots	340 g	12 oz	¾ lb
Courgettes (zucchini)	340 g	12 oz	¾ lb
Unsalted butter	100 g	4 oz	½ cup
Fresh coriander leaves or parsley, chopped	25 g	2 tbsp	2 tbsp
Salt and freshly ground black pepper to taste			

Scrape the carrots and wash the courgettes. Cut into julienne strips. These are about the size of fat matchsticks. This can be quickly done in a food processor fitted with a julienne or potato chipper attachment. Place the carrots and the courgettes in the basket of a steamer making sure that the carrots are on the bottom layer. The recipe can be prepared a few hours ahead to this point and steamed when needed.

Melt the butter in a separate pan and add the chopped herbs.

Place the basket over 1.2 cm/½ in salted water. Cover. Steam the vegetables for 12–15 minutes. They are done when the vegetables are tender but not too soft. Turn the vegetables into a serving dish and sprinkle with salt and pepper. Pour the herb butter over them. Serve immediately.

BROCCOLI AUX GRAINES DE SÉSAME

Broccoli with Sesame Seeds

There are many French dishes that can be seen to be based on Chinese cuisine. This is especially true since the advent of new light French cooking. Expeditions to China have influenced techniques, as with this quick and easy dish. Chinese stir frying maintains the natural colour and flavour of the green vegetable. The sesame seeds provide a contrasting texture and flavour.

Cooking time: 10 minutes To serve: 6

INGREDIENTS	METRIC	IMPERIAL	AMERICAN
Fresh broccoli	450 g	1 lb	1 lb
Butter	25 g	1 oz	2 tbsp
Oil	25 ml	1 fl oz	2 tbsp
Sesame seeds	25 g	2 tbsp	2 tbsp

Wash the broccoli and slice in 2.5 cm/1 in lengths. The effect is prettier if you slice the shoots on the diagonal. Blanch: fill a pot with water and bring to the boil; add the broccoli; as soon as the water comes back to the boil, drain; run cold water over the broccoli to stop the cooking and set the green colour.

Place the sesame seeds on a baking tray and place in the oven to brown. This will take about 5 minutes. Heat the oil and butter together in a frying pan. When the fat is sizzling, toss the broccoli in it. Let fry for a few minutes to cook the broccoli but keep them crisp. Add salt and pepper to taste. Place in a serving dish and sprinkle with the toasted sesame seeds. Serve immediately.

HINT: The broccoli can be blanched in advance and then quickly fried just before serving.

HARICOTS VERTS
Green Beans French Style

Choose young, small and firm green beans. They should all be approximately the same size and should have a good green colour, without mould. These beans are so sweet that I prefer them quickly cooked and served without a sauce. It is a shame to cook these special vegetables until they lose their colour and are soggy in texture. Although this is a simple recipe, I have included it because so many people are not shown how to cook these beans properly.

Cooking time: 4–7 minutes To serve: 6

INGREDIENTS	METRIC	IMPERIAL	AMERICAN
Small, young green beans	450 g	1 lb	1 lb
Butter	25 g	1 oz	1 oz
TO GARNISH:			
Butter	50 g	2 oz	¼ cup
Fresh parsley, or coriander, or chervil, chopped to sprinkle on top, approximately	25 g	2 tbsp	2 tbsp
Salt and freshly ground black pepper to taste			

Tip and tail the beans. If they are young, they will not need to have the string removed. Blanch: fill a pan with water and bring to the boil; place the beans in the boiling water; as soon as the water comes back to the boil, drain the beans and pour cold water over them to stop the cooking and set the green colour.

Melt the butter in a frying pan and toss the beans in the butter to make them crisp and finish the cooking. This will take approximately 2 minutes. If you like them less crisp, toss them for 5 minutes. Salt and pepper to taste.

Melt the rest of the butter and add the fresh herbs. Place the beans in a serving dish and pour the herb butter over them. Serve immediately.

HINT: The beans may be blanched in advance and then sautéed just before serving.

GRATIN DE FENOUIL
Fennel with Cheese

Fennel is a pale, bulb-shaped vegetable, that has a slight aniseed flavour. It is well known in France and Italy. It can be served uncooked as part of a salad, or cooked, and is delicious either way.

Cooking time: 45 minutes To serve: 6

INGREDIENTS	METRIC	IMPERIAL	AMERICAN
Fennel, medium sized	4	4	4
Butter	50 g	2 oz	¼ cup
Gruyère cheese, grated	75 g	3 oz	¾ cup

Wash the fennel and cut off any leafy growths at the top. Slice the fennel in half lengthwise. Place in water, cover and bring to the boil. Boil for 15 minutes or until the fennel is tender. Take out and drain. Slice lengthwise again in the same direction so that you are left with 1.2 cm/½ in slices.

To bake

Pre-heat the oven to 180°C/350°F/gas mark 4. Butter an ovenproof serving or gratin dish. Lay the fennel overlapping in the dish. Sprinkle with the cheese and place in the oven for 20 minutes. The fennel should be soft and the cheese melted and slightly golden.

HINT: The recipe can be prepared in advance, but do not place in the oven. Bake it 20 minutes before it is needed.

CONCOMBRES AUX HERBES
Glazed Cucumbers

Cucumbers are usually considered a salad vegetable. However, the French cook most vegetables, which gives them an entirely different texture and flavour. Sweet fresh cucumbers are quite delicious glazed and are certainly worth a try.

Cooking time: 15–20 minutes To serve: 6

INGREDIENTS	METRIC	IMPERIAL	AMERICAN
Cucumbers	5 large	5 large	5 large
Water	350 ml	12 fl oz	1½ cups
Butter	140 g	5 oz	½ cup + 1 tbsp
Salt and freshly ground black pepper to taste			
Fresh chervil, dill, or parsley, chopped	25 g	2 tbsp	2 tbsp

Peel the cucumber and slice in half lengthwise. Scrape out the seeds with a spoon. Cut in strips about 2.5 cm/1 in by 5 cm/2 in. Place in a heavy-bottomed saucepan and add the water, butter and a little salt and pepper. Do not add too much seasoning as it will become concentrated as the liquid reduces. Cook with half a lid over a medium heat for 10–15 minutes or until the cucumbers are tender. Remove the lid and simmer until nearly all the liquid is evaporated.

Sprinkle with the chopped herbs and adjust the seasoning to taste. Turn into a serving dish and serve.

HINT: These may be prepared a few hours before serving, do not add the herbs. Warm gently and add the herbs just before serving.

PETITS POIS À LA FRANÇAISE
Fricassée of Spring Vegetables

This recipe is always a delight, as it heralds the coming of spring. Fresh young peas, sweet baby carrots, and new hearts of lettuce all combine together to make this a treat. The best results are obtained with new spring vegetables.

Cooking time: 40–45 minutes To serve: 6

INGREDIENTS	METRIC	IMPERIAL	AMERICAN
Unshelled baby peas	2 kg	4½ lb	4½ lb
Baby spring carrots	450 g	1 lb	1 lb
Lettuce hearts	6	6	6
2 bunches spring onions			
Butter	50 g	2 oz	¼ cup
Water	225 ml	8 fl oz	1 cup
Castor sugar	50 g	2 oz	¼ cup
Salt	5 g	1 tsp	1 tsp
Salt and freshly ground black pepper to taste			

Shell the peas, scrape the small carrots and leave them whole. Wash the hearts of lettuce leaving them whole. Cut off the green stem of the spring onions, peel the skin and scrape the tip of the bulb. Leave them whole. Melt the butter in a heavy-bottomed casserole and add the peas, carrots and onions. Sauté for 2–3 minutes. Add the water and sugar and 5 g/one tsp of salt. Add the lettuce. Cover and cook over a low heat for 40 minutes or until the carrots can be pierced with a knife. Add salt and pepper to taste. Serve immediately.

Petits Pois à la Française

RATATOUILLE
Tomato, Aubergine and Courgette Casserole

A good ratatouille has the aroma of Provence. All of the ingredients are produced abundantly in this area of France and this recipe happily combines them. Every Frenchman has his own preparation. I like each vegetable to retain its own character and shape rather than mixing together into the sauce as one. Since this is a strong dish, it goes best with plain roasted or grilled meat or chicken. It tastes even better made a day in advance.

Cooking time: approximately 45 minutes To serve: 6–8

INGREDIENTS	METRIC	IMPERIAL	AMERICAN
Aubergines (egg plant), one	225 g	8 oz	2 cups
Courgettes (zucchini)	225 g	8 oz	2 cups
Onions, sliced	2 med	2 med	2 med
Olive oil	40 ml	3 tbsp	3 tbsp
Garlic, crushed	2 cloves	2 cloves	2 cloves
Tomatoes	680 g	1½ lb	1½ lb
Bouquet garni (branch fresh thyme, a few stalks parsley, 1 bay leaf, tied together in a bundle)			
Sugar	10 g	2 tsp	2 tsp
Green peppers, sliced	2	2	2
Salt and freshly ground black pepper to taste			

Peel the aubergine and cut into chunks about 5 cm/2 in in width.

Wash the courgettes and cut off the two ends. Cut into slices about 2.5 cm/1 in thick. Sprinkle these two vegetables with salt and leave to drain in a colander for 30 minutes.

HINT: This method removes the bitter liquids from the aubergine and courgettes and prevents them from absorbing too much oil during cooking.

To make the tomato sauce
Sweat the onions in a little of the oil until they are transparent. Add the garlic, quarter the tomatoes and add to the onions. Add the bouquet garni, cover and gently simmer for 10 minutes or until a sauce is formed. Sieve the sauce, pushing as much pulp through as possible, or remove the bouquet garni and purée in a food processor. The sauce should be thick. If it isn't simply put it back in the saucepan and reduce until thick. Add the sugar and salt and pepper to taste. Set aside.

To cook the other vegetables
Rinse the aubergines and courgettes, drain and pat dry. Heat the olive oil in a large frying pan and sauté the aubergines, one layer at a time, for about 2 minutes until they are lightly brown. Remove the aubergine and sauté the courgettes in the same way. Remove the courgettes and sauté the green peppers for about 1 minute.

To finish
Place the tomato sauce and vegetables in a heavy-bottomed casserole. Cover and simmer over medium heat for 10 minutes. Uncover and continue to cook until any excess liquid has evaporated (about 10–15 minutes more). The vegetables should be coated in tomato sauce but not swimming in it. Add salt and pepper to taste.

To serve
This dish may be served hot or cold. It can be made a day ahead and re-warmed. Be careful when re-warming not to scorch the bottom of the pan. Tomatoes burn easily.

HINT: Although this dish takes some time to prepare. I find that the result is well worth it. I usually make at least double the quantity and freeze what I don't need. Also, by adding some water to any leftovers, you can make a delicious soup.

POMMES DE TERRE À LA VAPEUR
Steamed New Potatoes

Sweet new potatoes are at their peak in June. However, one can now buy them from just after Christmas. They are so delicate that serving them with parsley and butter is all that is needed to provide a complementary addition to your main meal. Try steaming them and adding some different herbs.

Cooking time: 10 minutes To serve: 6

INGREDIENTS	METRIC	IMPERIAL	AMERICAN
New potatoes	450 g	1 lb	1 lb
Butter	50 g	2 oz	¼ cup
Fresh coriander leaves, or chervil, or parsley, chopped	40 g	3 tbsp	3 tbsp
TO GARNISH:			
Smoked streaky bacon (optional)	175 g	6 oz	¾ cup

To prepare the garnish
Place the bacon on a rack and place in a roasting tin in the oven at 180°C/350°F/gas mark 4. Bake until crisp and all of the fat has cooked away. This will take about 20 minutes. When it is crisp, take out and drain on a kitchen towel. Break up.

To cook the potatoes
Wash the potatoes but do not peel. Slice them 0.6 cm/¼ in thick. This may be done in a food processor. Place them in the basket of a steamer. Fill the bottom of the steamer with 1.2 cm/½ in of salted water. In a separate pan melt the butter and add the chopped herbs. Steam the potatoes for 10–15 minutes or until soft. Place them in a serving dish and add the melted butter and herbs. Add salt and pepper to taste. Toss very gently being careful not to break the slices. Sprinkle the bacon bits on top and serve.

PURÉE DE LÉGUMES
Winter Vegetable Purée

Vegetable purées have become a French favourite. In many restaurants they serve several kinds with varying tastes and colours. It is an interesting and different way to serve vegetables. Small amounts are used to garnish another vegetable or sometimes little tartlets are filled with purées. The golden colour of this recipe makes it a pretty accompaniment.

Cooking time: 1 hour To serve: 6–8

INGREDIENTS	METRIC	IMPERIAL	AMERICAN
Turnips	680 g	1½ lb	1½ lb
Potatoes	450 g	1 lb	1 lb
Carrots	680 g	1½ lb	1½ lb
Salt	15 g	1 tbsp	1 tbsp
Butter	75 g	3 oz	⅓ cup
Light brown sugar	50 g	2 oz	¼ cup
Nutmeg approx.	10 g	2 tsp	2 tsp
Salt and white pepper to taste			

Peel the turnips and potatoes and cut into 2.5 cm/1 in chunks. Place in a large pan with cold water to cover. Bring to the boil, cover and simmer for 30 minutes. Peel the carrots and cut into chunks, add to the turnips and potatoes with 15 g/1 tbs salt. Cover and simmer for 30 minutes until all the vegetables are tender. Drain. Place the vegetables back in the pan and place them over the heat. Cover. Shake the pan until the vegetables are dry. Purée the vegetables in a food processor or pass through the fine sieve of a food mill. Add the butter, sugar, nutmeg and salt and pepper to taste.

To serve
Serve the purée as it is, with the main course, placed in little tartlets or on a bed of fresh spinach leaf. This dish may be made in advance and re-warmed.

AUBERGINES À LA TOMATE

Aubergines with Tomato Sauce

The combination of aubergine and tomato is used successfully in many cuisines. This recipe may be served hot or cold or re-warmed. I usually prepare it in advance and then gently re-warm the aubergines in the oven. It is especially nice with beef or lamb or can be served on its own as a first course.

Cooking time: 20 minuts To serve: 6

INGREDIENTS	METRIC	IMPERIAL	AMERICAN
Aubergine (egg plant)	1 large	1 large	1 large
Oil for frying	40 ml	3 tbsp	3 tbsp
Plain flour	25 g	2 tbsp	2 tbsp
FOR THE SAUCE:			
Olive oil	15 ml	1 tbsp	1 tbsp
Onion, chopped	1 small	1 small	1 small
Garlic, crushed	1 clove	1 clove	1 clove
Ripe tomatoes	4–5 large	4–5 large	4–5 large
Bouquet garni (2 branches fresh thyme, a few stalks parsley, bay leaf).			
Tomato purée (paste) (optional)	5 ml	1 tsp	1 tsp
TO GARNISH:			
Black olives (12 olives or enough to decorate the aubergine slices.)	175 g	6 oz	1½ cups
Fresh parsley, chopped	25 g	2 tbsp	2 tbsp
Salt and freshly ground black pepper to taste			

Wash the aubergine and trim on either end. Leaving the skin on, cut into round slices about 1.2 cm/½ in thick. Sprinkle the slices with salt and score on each side. Place the slices on a baking tray and place another weighted tray on top. Leave for 30 minutes.

HINT: This method removes the bitter liquids from the aubergines and prevents them from absorbing too much oil during cooking.

To make the tomato sauce

Pour the olive oil in a saucepan and sweat the onions until transparent. Add the garlic and sauté for 1 minute. Quarter the tomatoes and add with the bouquet garni to the pan. Cover and gently simmer for 10 minutes or until a sauce is formed. Sieve the sauce, pushing as much pulp as possible through the sieve, or remove the bouquet garni and purée in a food processor. The sauce should be thick. If it isn't, simply put it back in the saucepan and reduce until thick. Add salt and pepper to taste.

HINT: If using winter tomatoes, add 15 g/1 tbs tomato purée.

To sauté the aubergines

Pre-heat the oven to 170°C/325°F/gas mark 3. Add some pepper to the flour. Pat the aubergine slices dry with kitchen towel. Dip the slices into the flour. Heat the oil in a large frying pan and lightly brown the slices on each side. Work with 2 or 3 at a time to ensure they do not burn. Drain on kitchen towel. Place on a baking sheet and place in the oven for 10 minutes.

To serve

Blanch the olives and remove the stones. Spread some warm tomato sauce on each slice of aubergine. Place 2 half olives in the centre of each slice and sprinkle with chopped parsley.

HINT: This dish may be prepared in advance. Leave the aubergine slices spread with the tomato sauce on a baking tray. Warm in the oven when needed. Add the olives and parsley just before serving.

(Clockwise) Gratin de Fenouil (p 119), Aubergines à la Tomate (p 125), Pommes de Terre à la Vapeur (p 123)

GRATIN DAUPHINOIS
Potatoes with Cheese, Onion and Milk

There are many versions of this well known French dish. Its fame is well deserved. I find this particular recipe to be delicious and always successful.

Cooking time: approximately 1 hour
To serve: 6

INGREDIENTS	METRIC	IMPERIAL	AMERICAN
Potatoes	900 g	2 lb	2 lb
Egg	1	1	1
Milk	150 ml	5 fl oz	$^2/_3$ cup
Onion, chopped	1 large	1 large	1 large
Salt and freshly ground black pepper to taste			
Cheddar cheese, grated	50 g	2 oz	½ cup
Garlic	1 clove	1 clove	1 clove
Butter	15 g	½ oz	1 tbsp
Gratin dish or oval ovenproof dish			

To prepare the gratin dish
Butter the bottom and sides of the dish and rub with a piece of the garlic clove. Sprinkle with salt and pepper.

To prepare the potatoes and filling
Peel the potatoes and thinly slice. This can be done in a food processor.
Place the egg into a bowl and break up with a fork. Warm the milk and add to the egg. Strain.

To assemble
Place one layer of potato slices in the gratin dish. Sprinkle with some chopped onion and salt and pepper. Place another layer of potatoes over the onions. Continue in this manner with onions, salt and pepper between each layer of potatoes. When the dish is full, make a neat spiral of potatoes covering the top. Pour the egg and milk mixture over the potatoes. Let the liquid seep down to the bottom of the dish. Sprinkle the grated cheese over the top.

To bake
Pre-heat the oven to 170°C/325°F/gas mark 3. Place the gratin dish in a roasting tin. Place the tin in the oven and three quarters fill it with boiling water.

HINT: It is easier to bring a kettle of boiling water to the tin in the oven than carry a roasting tin with boiling water to the oven.

Bake for about 1 hour. The top should be crusty and golden and the potatoes soft.

NAVETS SAUTÉS
Sautéed Turnips

This method of cooking turnips makes them suitable to accompany any main dish. They are available in winter or spring, and as prepared here can substitute for potato, carrots, or any of the onion family. If you can find the small baby turnips, so much the better.

Cooking time: 20–30 minutes To serve: 6

INGREDIENTS	METRIC	IMPERIAL	AMERICAN
Turnips	900 g	2 lb	2 lb
Butter	75 g	3 oz	$^1/_3$ cup
Castor sugar	25 g	2 tbsp	2 tbsp
Salt and freshly ground black pepper to taste			

Peel the turnips and cut in 1.2 cm/½ in cubes. Melt the butter in a saucepan. When the butter is smoking, add the turnip cubes. Stir constantly for 2 minutes. Lower the flame and let sauté uncovered, stirring occasionally. Sauté for about 20 minutes. They should be tender when pierced with a knife, and golden brown. If they are not yet tender add 25 ml/2 tbs water and continue to sauté. When they are ready, add the sugar, salt and pepper. Stir. Serve.

SALSIFIS
Salsify

This root vegetable is white inside and covered with black-brown skin. It is sweet, available in the winter time and makes a welcome change from the usual winter vegetables.

Cooking time: 15–20 minutes To serve: 6

INGREDIENTS	METRIC	IMPERIAL	AMERICAN
Salsify	900 g	2 lb	2 lb
Water to cover			
Lemon juice or vinegar	15 ml	1 tbsp	1 tbsp
Butter	50 g	2 oz	1¼ cups
Salt and freshly ground black pepper to taste			
TO GARNISH:			
Fresh parsley, chopped	25 g	2 tbsp	2 tbsp

Peel the salsify and wash thoroughly. Cut into 2.5 cm/1 in pieces. Place in a bowl of water with lemon juice or vinegar. This will keep it from going dark. Drain and place in a pan of cold water. Cover and bring to the boil. Simmer for 15–20 minutes until tender. Melt the butter in a separate pan. Add the parsley. Drain the salsify and place in a serving bowl. Season to taste. Pour the herb butter over it. Serve immediately.

GRATIN DE CHOU ET DE RIZ
Rice and Cabbage with Cheese

The method of cooking the cabbage in this recipe takes away the strong taste or smell sometimes connected with this vegetable. With the cheese and rice this dish is almost a meal in itself. It makes a good luncheon dish or family supper on its own.

Cooking time: 30–40 minutes To serve: 6

INGREDIENTS	METRIC	IMPERIAL	AMERICAN
½ head of cabbage, approximately	450 g	1 lb	1 lb
(The curly-leafed cabbage is best, but the smooth-leafed may be used.)			
Butter	25 g	1 oz	2 tbsp
Rice, washed	25 g	2 tbsp	2 tbsp
Salt	8 g	½ tbsp	½ tbsp
Cheese, Cheddar or Gruyère, grated	50 g	2 oz	½ cup
Crème fraîche	80 ml	6 tbsp	6 tbsp
Salt and freshly ground pepper to taste			

To cook the cabbage
Take the leaves off the head off the cabbage and wash. Bring a large pan of water to the boil and add the leaves. Boil for 10 minutes. Drain and pour cold water over the cabbage. Drain again. Chop coarsely. This can be done on a board or in a food processor.

To cook with the rice
Melt the butter in a large saucepan and add the rice, chopped cabbage and 8 g/½ tbs salt. Sauté for 1 minute. Pour enough water into the pan just to cover the rice and cabbage. Cover and simmer 20 minutes. The rice should be cooked and no water should remain.

HINT: If all the liquid is absorbed and the rice is not cooked, add more liquid. If the rice is cooked but there is still excess water take the cover off and let the moisture evaporate.

Season the rice to your taste. Butter an oven-proof serving dish and place the rice in it. (The dish can be made ahead to this point.) Sprinkle the cheese on top and cook for 20 minutes at 180°C/350°F/gas mark 4

To serve
Serve when hot and the cheese on top is golden and crusty. Pour a spoonful of crème fraîche over each hot serving.

DESSERTS

DESSERTS

DESSERTS

Desserts hold an important place at our table and make a very agreeable finish to our dinners. Young or old, on special diets or not, everyone looks forward to, and enjoys this part of the meal.

In the eighteenth and nineteenth centuries desserts, often the fifth course, were presented in great style. The tables were filled with set pieces fashioned in pastry and set on the table at the beginning of the meal as a decoration. When it came time for the dessert the table was filled with sweets of all kinds, meticulously selected to harmonise with the set pieces. Today, although less ostentatious, our desserts are still sumptuous and beautiful. I have tried in this section to make a selection from the range of possibilities: tarts, cakes, fruits and creams, and the not-to-be-forgotten chocolate dreams. I hope you will find something to suit your taste.

Here are a few hints to help you towards success:

1 When planning a meal, I try to plan the dessert to go with the entire menu. Thus, I use a light or fruit based dessert with a rich or heavy meal. Or if the meal is light then a richer dessert is in order. It is usually a good idea to give a choice of some type of fruit along with whatever other delight you serve. Although, I must admit that the fruit is very often passed over in favour of the special treat.

2 For cakes:

a The harder you work your eggs the lighter your cake will be. Thus, if the recipe tells you to work the eggs and sugar until light and fluffy, this means until the colour is white and the volume has increased.

b Your cakes will easily come out of their tins if you prepare the tin properly. This means to cut a piece of greaseproof paper to fit the bottom of the tin. Melt some fat and brush the bottom with the fat. Place the paper in the tin. Brush the entire inside including the paper with the fat. Sprinkle castor sugar to cover the inside. Sprinkle a small amount of flour in the bottom. Shake out any excess.

c There are several rules to go by to know when a cake is ready:
- The sides begin to shrink away from the tin;
- touching the top does not leave a finger print and it feels bouncy;
- a small knife inserted in the centre comes out clean.

When you test your cake, do not bring it out of the oven or even slide the rack out. The cool air will cause the top to fall if it is not quite done. You will have an indentation in the top.

3 For desserts with gelatine:
Make sure the gelatine is completely dissolved. Before you start your recipe, sprinkle the gelatine onto the liquid required and place it in a pan of hot water. It will dissolve as you prepare the other ingredients. Be careful not to bring gelatine to the boil as it will loose its gelling properties.

4 For caramel:

When making caramel be sure that all of the sugar is dissolved before the water is brought to the boil. Otherwise, the sugar will harden and burn in spots ruining the final flavour.

5 To melt chocolate:

Chocolate must be melted carefully. It is best to set it in a pan over hot water and turn the heat off while the chocolate melts. If chocolate is overheated, the butter fat will separate and then harden in different colours. Chocolate must either be melted completely dry or with the exact amount of water or liquid required by the recipe. Do not let any steam get into the melting chocolate.

6 Folding in:

Many desserts ask for one mixture to be folded into another. A general rule to remember is that the mixtures should be of equal consistency for them to fold in evenly. Thus a spoonful of whipped egg whites are put into the accompanying sauce to soften it before folding in the rest. Cream is half whipped to meet the texture of a custard.

MOUSSE LÉGÈRE AU CHOCOLAT AMER
Light Chocolate Mousse

Eating this mousse is like biting into a chocolate cloud. It is made without cream, butter or egg yolks so the pure chocolate flavour predominates. The secret of this recipe is to beat up your whites properly and fold in the rest of the ingredients carefully.

Preparation time: 20 minutes To serve: 6

INGREDIENTS	METRIC	IMPERIAL	AMERICAN
Bitter chocolate (sometimes called dry chocolate)	125 g	4½ oz	4½ oz
Unsweetened cocoa powder	15 g	½ oz	1 tbsp
Strong black coffee	40 ml	3 tbsp	3 tbsp
Egg whites	8	8	8
Pinch of salt			
Castor sugar	50 g	2 oz	¼ cup

To melt the chocolate

Break the chocolate into pieces and place in a bain marie with the cocoa and coffee. Melt gently over hot water. When it is melted stir well until it is thoroughly blended. Remove from the heat.

To beat the whites

Beat the egg whites with a pinch of salt. When they have reached a medium peak (the whites will form a peak but not a firm one) add 1 tbs of the sugar and continue to beat until the whites form a stiff peak. Fold in the rest of the sugar. Be careful not to overfold, you want to leave as much air as possible in the whites.

To finish

Take a large spoonful of the whites and mix them into the chocolate to lighten it.

HINT: It is easier to fold two mixtures together if they are near to the same consistency. Thus, the chocolate needs to be made lighter.

Fold the chocolate into the egg whites. Turn into a souffle dish or any type of serving bowl. Refrigerate for at least 1 hour.

To serve

This mousse is best eaten on the day it is made. But, it can certainly be prepared several hours in advance. Bring to the table and scoop out each serving. It may be prepared in individual ramekins. If you wish, the top can be decorated with rosettes of whipped cream.

CRÈME RENVERSÉE
Creme Caramel

The French and Spainish both claim this dish. The actual winners of the contest are the people who have the pleasure of eating this light, smooth and tasty cream. Try it as a companion to fresh fruit such as strawberries, kiwi, or poached pears.

Cooking time: 45 minutes To serve: 6

INGREDIENTS	METRIC	IMPERIAL	AMERICAN
Sugar cubes	70 g	2½ oz	½ cup
Water to moisten the cubes plus 1 tbsp			
FOR CREAM:			
Milk	475 ml	17 fl oz	2 cups+ 1 tbsp
Castor sugar	70 g	2½ oz	¼ cup+ 1 tbsp
1 vanilla pod or 1 teaspoon extract			
Eggs	3	3	3
Charlotte mould, soufflé dish 600 ml/20 fl oz size, or individual ramekins			

Pre-heat oven to 190°C/375°F/gas mark 5

To caramelise a metal mould: (see instructions below for a non-metal mould)
Place the sugar cubes in the mould and moisten each one. Spoon water over them until they are wet and then add 15 ml/1 tbs water. Place over the heat and dissolve the sugar completely. After the sugar is dissolved, bring the liquid to the boil and cook until it reaches a caramel or light golden brown colour. Using kitchen tongs immediately plunge the bottom of the mould into cold water to stop the cooking. Do not worry if it hisses. Roll the syrup around the sides of the mould until it is coated. Set aside to harden completely. Use the same process for each ramekin if making individual ones.

HINT: The caramel for a non-metal mould must be made in the same way in a saucepan and quickly poured into the mould. You must work quickly once the sugar has turned to caramel. You want the bottom and sides of the mould to be coated with caramel. Set aside to harden completely.

To make the cream
Warm the milk with the vanilla pod and sugar. Dissolve the sugar and then cool. Remove the pod.

Beat the eggs in a bowl and pour the flavoured milk slowly into the eggs. Be careful not to pour too fast or you will curdle the eggs. Pour into the caramelised mould. Place the mould in a bain marie or roasting tin. Pour boiling water into the bain marie to reach three quarters of the way up the mould. Place in the oven.

The crème caramel should take 45 minutes to cook and is done when it is firm. A knife inserted in the centre will come out clean. It may be slightly browned on top. Take it out and cool. Slip a knife round the top edges and turn out onto a plate.

This recipe can be made ahead and turned out of the mould. The caramel will come out as a liquid covering the cream.

To serve
Slice or spoon the cream onto each dish and spoon some sauce over it.

SOUFFLÉ AU GRAND MARNIER

Grand Marnier Soufflé

Here is a cold soufflé made without gelatine. It is made and frozen and then slightly softened before serving. It is an elegant dish that will keep for a few weeks in your freezer.

Preparation time: 30 minutes To serve: 6

INGREDIENTS	METRIC	IMPERIAL	AMERICAN
Eggs	3	3	3
Egg yolk	1	1	1
Sugar	100 g	4 oz	½ cup
Trifle sponges	6	6	6
Grand Marnier	120 ml	4 fl oz	½ cup
Orange zest, grated skin from orange	1	1	1
Whipping (heavy) cream	300 ml	10 fl oz	1¼ cup
TO GARNISH:			
Icing (confectioner's) sugar	25 g	1 oz	2 tbsp
Powdered unsweetened cocoa	25 g	1 oz	2 tbsp
Soufflé dish, approximately 18 cm/7 in diameter, 10 cm/4 in deep			
Greaseproof paper			
String			

To prepare the soufflé dish

Cut a piece of greaseproof paper to fit around the dish and extend above the rim to form a collar. Tie the paper tightly in place.

HINT: Holding the paper in place while trying to tie some string tightly around can be tricky. A paper clip is a useful aid. Fit the paper around the dish and clip it together at the top edge. This will leave you with two hands to tie the string.

To make the soufflé

With an electric whisk beat the eggs with the yolk and the sugar in a bowl, until a ribbon forms. This should take about 20 minutes. Lift the beaters and make a W, if this remains then a ribbon stage has been reached. This is an important step. The volume will be tripled, and the mixture will form the base of the soufflé.

While the eggs are being whipped, cut the trifle sponges into small cubes, pour half of the Grand Marnier over them and let them absorb the liquid. Add the zest of orange to the eggs. Half whip the cream adding the remaining Grand Marnier as you do. Fold the cream and trifle sponges into the egg mixture. Pour into the soufflé dish and place in the freezer immediately. It must be a freezer that has a low temperature. Once frozen use cling film to cover the top surface of the soufflé.

To serve

Take the soufflé out of the freezer about 30 minutes before you wish to serve it and place in the refrigerator. It should be slightly soft, not rock hard when you serve it. Sprinkle the icing sugar mixed with cocoa powder on the top. Remove the collar and spoon out individual servings. (It may also be frozen in the same manner in individual ramekins.)

HINT: If you have a frost free freezer, then the soufflé will be softer and will not need as much time to soften.

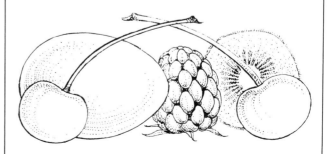

OEUFS À LA NEIGE
Floating Islands

This traditional French dessert is always welcome and very light. Whenever I have people coming round at short notice, I can always whip this up because it is easy and the ingredients: eggs, sugar, milk, and vanilla are usually in the house.

Cooking time: 30 minutes To serve: 6

INGREDIENTS	METRIC	IMPERIAL	AMERICAN
Milk	500 ml	18 fl oz	2¼ cups
Sugar	75 g	3 oz	⅓ cup
Vanilla pod	1	1	1
Eggs	4	4	4
FOR GARNISH:			
Slivered almonds	50 g	2 oz	¼ cup
Cubed sugar for caramel	70 g	2½ oz	½ cup
Water to moisten the cubes plus 1 tbsp			

To poach the egg whites

In a medium sized saucepan, warm the milk with the sugar and vanilla pod. Completely dissolve the sugar. After the sugar has dissolved, remove the vanilla pod. Separate the eggs. Whisk the egg whites to a stiff peak. Gently spoon the whites on top of the milk. Boil the milk until the whites float to the top of the pan. Take off the heat and with 2 large spoons turn them over. Place back on the heat and boil again until the whites rise. Take off the heat and spoon the whites onto a plate. Make six large mounds on the plate.

HINT: The best way is to spoon out 6 large mounds from the saucepan trying to give them a peaked top. If you have difficulty with this, don't worry, simply spoon any stray bits onto the mounds as you make them. They will stay put and look fine.

The poached whites will drain on the plate.
To make the crème anglaise or custard

Break up the yolks in a large bowl. Very slowly pour the milk used to poach the whites into the yolks, stirring constantly. If you pour too fast you will curdle the yolks. Pour the mixture back into the saucepan and place over a low heat. Stir constantly until the milk begins to thicken and becomes a cream. This will take about 10 minutes. The cream will coat the back of a spoon. Place the pan in cold water and continue to stir until it cools. Many custards are curdled at this point because they continue to cook in their own heat in the pan even though they are off the fire. Strain into a serving bowl.

To make the garnish

Place the almonds on a baking tray in the oven to brown the edges. Be very careful not to burn them. Take them out and sprinkle on the whites.

To make the caramel

Place the cubed sugar in a heavy-bottomed pan. Spoon water over each cube to moisten it completely and then add 15 ml/1 tbs water to the pan. Dissolve the sugar over a low flame. When the sugar is completely dissolved, bring the liquid to a boil and cook until it forms a caramel or light, golden brown colour. Immediately take the pan off the heat and allow the caramel to drip from the spoon down the sides of the mounds of whites.

To serve

Carefully lift the islands off the plate and float them on the custard. Give each person an island and spoon custard around it. This dish can be made in the morning for the evening, but do not make the caramel until about 1 hour before serving.

Oeufs à la Neige

BAVAROIS AUX FRAMBOISES
Raspberry Bavarian Cream

Bavarois seemed to have gone out of fashion for a time. With the advent of new light cooking, however, they have come into their own again. In fact a *bavarois* is actually a custard or crème anglaise that is set with a little gelatine. This recipe is made with raspberries. Any type of fruit can be used. Multicoloured bavarois can be made by dividing the mixture and adding chocolate, coffee or fruit purées to the custard. This is a lovely summer dish and can be made ahead.

Preparation time: 20 minutes To serve: 6–8

INGREDIENTS	METRIC	IMPERIAL	AMERICAN
Water	40 ml	3 tbsp	3 tbsp
Gelatine	15 g	½ oz	1 tbsp
Milk	600 ml	1 pt	2½ cups
Vanilla pod	1	1	1
Egg yolks	4	4	4
Castor sugar	40 g	3 tbsp	3 tbsp
Double (heavy) cream	50 ml	2 fl oz	¼ cup
Raspberries, hulled and washed or defrosted if frozen	120 ml	4 oz	½ cup
Mould (Any type will do. French tables used to be filled with different types of intricate moulds.) 850 ml/1½ pt/3¾ cups capacity			
A little oil to oil the mould			
FOR SAUCE:			
Raspberries (hulled and washed or defrosted if frozen)	250 g	9 oz	2¼ cups
Icing (confectioner's) sugar	70 g	2½ oz	¼ cup + 1 tbsp
Kirsch	40 ml	3 tbsp	3 tbsp

Lightly oil the mould. This is best done by wetting your fingers with some oil and rubbing them over the inside of the mould. This should leave a satiny finish with no drops of oil. Set aside.

Pour the water into a small heavy-bottomed saucepan and sprinkle the gelatine over it. Let stand in a pan of hot water or over a low heat until dissolved. Do not bring to the boil or it will lose its gelling properties.

To make the cream
Scald the milk with the vanilla pod. Cool. Cream the egg yolks and sugar. Beat the mixture until the eggs turn white. (This can be done with an electric beater). Take the vanilla pod out and slowly pour the milk into the egg mixture stirring constantly. If the milk is still hot and you pour too quickly, the eggs will curdle. Pour the mixture back into the saucepan and cook over a low heat to thicken to a custard. This may take about 10 minutes. It will coat the back of a spoon when thickened. Pour into a bowl and continue to stir until cool.

HINT: When making custard, I usually have a shallow pan of cold water nearby. If I find the sauce starting to curdle, I quickly plunge the bottom of the saucepan into the cold water. This will save the sauce.

To add the gelatine
Make sure that the gelatine is completely dissolved. Pour the gelatine into the cooled custard. Mix thoroughly. Half whip the cream. It should be about the same consistency as the custard. Fold the cream into the custard. As the custard starts to gel, pour a little into the mould.

HINT: The custard will gel sooner if you place the bowl in a pan or bowl filled with ice and water. Thus, each layer will be partially set before the next goes in and the raspberries will not sink to the bottom. But, you must work quickly using this method.

Add some of the raspberries and then another layer of custard. Continue in this manner making sure the last layer is custard. Cover with cling film and refrigerate until set. This will take at least 3 hours.

To make the sauce

Purée the raspberries either in a food processor, liquidiser, or food mill, and pass through a sieve. Sift in the icing sugar and stir in the kirsch. Taste for sweetness. Add more sugar or kirsch if necessary. Be careful not to overpower the flavour with too much kirsch.

To finish

Slip a knife around the edge of the mould. Loosen the edges and turn out onto a serving plate.

> *HINT: There is an air lock that forms in the mould and you must break this to release the bavarois. Try to pull it away carefully from the sides to let air into the mould. Another method is to place the entire mould including the top in a sink filled with warm water. Take out quickly and dry the top with some kitchen paper. Turn out immediately.*

> *HINT: Dampen the serving plate with water before turning out the bavarois. This will enable you to move the bavarois to the centre once it has been turned out.*

To serve

Pour the sauce around the bavarois and serve.

AVOCAT EN SURPRISE
Avocado Surprise

Although avocados are usually served as a first course, this special blend of flavours makes an intriguing dessert that will surprise and please your guests. Don't mention what it is before they taste! The flavour of this dish depends on a balance of the avocado and lime flavours.

Preparation time: 10–15 minutes To serve: 6

INGREDIENTS	METRIC	IMPERIAL	AMERICAN
Ripe avocados	2	2	2
Limes	2	2	2
Fresh mint, chopped approx.	25 g	2 tbsp	2 tbsp
FOR SUGAR SYRUP:			
Castor sugar	250 g	9 oz	1 cup+ 1 tbsp
Water	300 ml	10 fl oz	1¼ cup
Kirsch or Grand Marnier	70 ml	2½ fl oz	⅓ cup

To make the syrup

Dissolve the sugar in the water over a low heat. When all the sugar is dissolved, bring the liquid to a boil. Do not boil before the sugar is completely dissolved. Boil for 5 mins. Do not let the syrup colour. Cool. Add the liqueur.

To finish

Mash the avocado and add some of the syrup. Scrape some of the lime skin (zest) into the mixture. Slice one of the limes in half and cut 6 thin slices for decoration. Set aside. Extract the juice from the other lime and the remainder of the first one. Add the lime juice and chopped mint to the avocado. Taste and add more syrup as necessary. The mixture will be the consistency of whipped cream and very green in colour.

To serve

Spoon into dessert dishes and place a slice of lime on the edge to decorate.

> *HINT: The sugar syrup can be made in advance and kept in the refrigerator. The avocado mixture can be whipped up in a food processor or strong liquidiser a few hours before serving. I find it is best to leave the finished mixture in a mixing bowl and then stir it a few times before placing it in the dessert dishes when it is needed.*

LE COEUR À LA CRÈME
Heart-shaped Cream

In France they serve this dish at buffet parties. The slightly tangy but sweet cheese provides a delightful accompaniment for strawberries. Leave the stems on the strawberries so guests can hold them and dip into the cheese. It can be made a day in advance.

Preparation time: 15 minutes To serve: 6–8

INGREDIENTS	METRIC	IMPERIAL	AMERICAN
Water	40 ml	3 tbsp	3 tbsp
Gelatine	15 g	½ oz	1 tbsp
Fromage blanc	450 g	1 lb	1 lb
Icing (confectioner's) sugar	40 g	3 tbsp	3 tbsp
Vanilla extract	5 ml	1 tsp	1 tsp
Double (heavy) cream	225 g	8 oz	1 cup
FOR THE GARNISH:			
Ripe strawberries	900 g	2 lbs	2 lbs
Heart shaped tin			
Greaseproof paper			

HINT: Fromage blanc is a French cheese that is made with either 40% or 0% fat. It is available in delicatessens, but a substitute may be made:

Cottage cheese	*225 g*	*8 oz*	*1 cup*
Plain yogurt	*250 g*	*9 fl oz*	*1 cup + 1 tbsp*
Lemon juice	*15 ml*	*1 tbsp*	*1 tbsp*

Mix all of these together in a food processor or liquidiser.

HINT: If possible, use vanilla extract. Vanilla essence does not provide the same taste.

Le Coeur à la Crème

To prepare the tin
Cut a piece of greaseproof paper to fit the bottom of the tin. Do not grease the tin. Set aside.

To melt the gelatine
Pour the water into a small pan. Sprinkle the gelatine on top. Place the pan in hot water and leave it until the gelatine is completely dissolved. Do not bring the gelatine to the boil or it will loose its gelling properties.

To make the cream
Beat the cheese until smooth and add the icing sugar. Add the vanilla. Taste. Add more vanilla or sugar if necessary. It should be slightly tangy. Pour the completely dissolved gelatine into the cheese mixture. Mix well. Half whip the cream so that it is the same consistency as the cheese. Mix into the cheese. Pour into the tin and refrigerate for half an hour. Place a piece of cling film over the top and refrigerate until ready to use.

To finish
Using a small knife or your finger, gently pull the edge of the cream away from the sides of the tin to create an air pocket. Turn out onto a large serving platter. Wash and dry the strawberries and place around the cream. Leave the stems so that they can be dipped into the cream. Cherries or other colourful fruit may also be used.

To serve
Spoon some of the cream onto each dish and serve some strawberries around it.

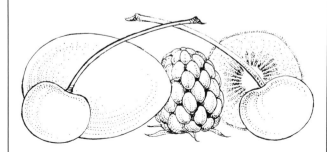

ORANGES AU CARAMEL
Oranges in Caramel

Serve colourful oranges sitting in a golden sauce and see how they bring a sparkle to your table. The syrup can be made ahead and the oranges prepared on the day they are needed.

Cooking time: 10–15 minutes To serve: 6

INGREDIENTS	METRIC	IMPERIAL	AMERICAN
Oranges	6	6	6
Castor sugar	175 g	6 oz	¾ cup
Cold water	150 ml	5 fl oz	⅔ cup
Warm water	225 ml	8 fl oz	1 cup
TO GARNISH:			
Orange needle shreds (enough to sprinkle a few over each orange)			
6 cocktail sticks			

To make the needle shreds and peel the oranges
To make the shreds, carefully peel off pieces of orange skin trying not to take any of the pith. This is best done with a potato peeler. Cut these into needle thin shreds and blanch in boiling water for 1 minute. Rinse in cold water. Wrap in a damp paper towel until needed. The shreds will keep overnight if placed in the towel in a plastic bag and refrigerated.

Using a serrated knife, cut with a sawing motion between the skin and flesh of the orange. Continue around in circles until the skin is removed. Try not to leave any pith.

To make the sauce
Dissolve the sugar in the cold water over a low heat. Be sure the water does not boil before all the sugar is dissolved. Bring the liquid to a boil and cook until a light caramel, or golden brown colour. Take off the flame and immediately pour the warm water into the caramel.

HINT: It is a good idea to wear an oven glove or wrap your hand in a tea towel when pouring the water into the caramel, as it can spatter and give you a nasty burn.

Replace the pan on the heat and stir to dissolve the hardened particles. Cool. This sauce will keep several days in the refrigerator.

To garnish
Partially slice the oranges into 6 slices across the membranes: with a serrated knife slice the orange nearly in half; make two slices nearly through the orange to the right, and two to the left of the centre slice leaving the slices still attached. Stand the orange on its end and pierce with a cocktail stick to hold together. Stand the oranges in a serving bowl and sprinkle with the needle shreds. Spoon the sauce over them.

To serve
Serve one orange per person in individual fruit bowls with some sauce poured over each one.

HINT: If serving a lot of people, the oranges can be sliced and placed in the sauce in a bowl. You will not need one per person in this case.

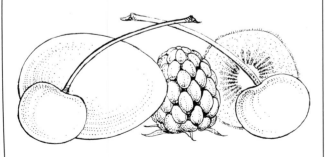

OMELETTE AUX BANANES
Banana Omelette

Dessert omelettes are light and fluffy and a wonderful change from the usual type of pudding. This is the type of dish you might serve at an informal supper with close friends who won't mind a slight delay in serving each person. The result is well worth the wait. You can also use this basic recipe to make savoury rather than sweet omelettes.

**Cooking time: 5–10 minutes To serve: 6
(Each omelette will serve 2 people.)**

INGREDIENTS	METRIC	IMPERIAL	AMERICAN
FOR OMELETTE:			
Eggs, size 2	6	6	6
Single cream	40 ml	3 tbsp	3 tbsp
Castor sugar	40 g	3 tbsp	3 tbsp
Unsalted butter	40 g	1½ oz	3 tbsp
FOR FILLING:			
Bananas	6	6	6
Unsalted butter	40 g	1½ oz	3 tbsp
Apricot jam	75 g	6 tbsp	6 tbsp
TO GARNISH:			
Sprinkling of icing (confectioner's) sugar			

To make filling
Peel the bananas and slice diagonally. Melt the butter in a frying pan and sauté the bananas gently, stirring with a fork. Add the jam to bind the bananas together. Keep warm on a very low heat while making the omelette.

To make one omelette
Separate 2 of the eggs. Mix the 2 yolks, 15 ml/ 1 tbs cream and 15 g/1 tbs sugar together. Whip the 2 eggs whites to a stiff peak. Mix a spoonful of the whites into the yolks to make them nearer to the consistency of the whites. Fold the yolk mixture into the whites. Heat an omelette pan with 15 g/½ oz butter. When the butter is foaming, pour in the eggs. Leave to set on the bottom.

Place the pan in a medium oven or under the grill for 1–2 minutes. Leave a little longer if you like a drier omelette. Turn the omelette out onto a serving plate. Spread ⅓ of the filling over half of the omelette. Fold the omelette in half over the filling and sprinkle the top with icing sugar.

To serve
Serve immediately. Cut in half and serve two portions. You may find it so light that one omelette per person is needed. Repeat the omelette preparation for the second and third omelettes.

HINT: The dish has been taught this way in my classes. Trying to prepare the entire omelette mixture in advance and dividing it in thirds does not work as well. In spite of having to make this at the last minute and serving each person as it is made, my students have told me that it is well worth the effort.

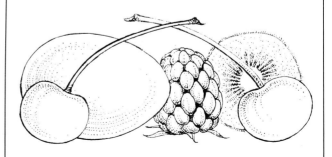

Sorbet au Piña Colada
Piña Colada Sorbet

Say piña colada and it brings to mind thoughts of palm trees, white sands, and blue ocean. This is a coconut based drink, made with rum, served in the tropics. The ingredients, without the rum, can be made into a sorbet. Served surrounded by exotic fruits, it's a wonderful way to bring some sun and cheer to a dinner party. The sorbet is made in a mechanical ice cream freezer, but works well made without one. Directions for both are given.

Preparation time: about 30 minutes To serve: 6–8

INGREDIENTS	METRIC	IMPERIAL	AMERICAN
Cream of coconut	175 ml	6 oz	¾ cup

This is sold in tins in many supermarkets and delicatessens. (Do not confuse it with creamed coconut which is sold in solid blocks.)

Unsweetened pineapple juice	250 ml	9 oz	1 cup + 2 tbsp

Juice of 1 small or ½ large lemon

Freezing salt, if using a mechanical freezer.

TO GARNISH

1 mango, 2 kiwi, 1 papaya, 2 bananas, or any fresh ripe fruit available such as grapes, strawberries, cherries etc. Fresh mint.

Mix the cream of coconut, pineapple juice and lemon juice together. Taste. It may be too sweet, in which case add more lemon juice.

Place in a mechanical freezer and freeze according to the directions. A sorbetier may also be used.

HINT: Be sure the dasher and container are free of all fat before using, by pouring boiling water over them.

When the sorbet begins to hold its shape, after about 30 minutes, place in a plastic container. Cover with a piece of greaseproof paper and a lid and freeze.

To make without a freezing machine

Simply mix the ingredients together and place in a metal tray or shallow metal bowl in the freezer. Take out every 20 minutes and beat. If you have a food processor, process the mixture after about 1 hour. When it begins to hold its form, you no longer need to beat it. Place in a plastic container. Cover with a piece of greaseproof paper and a lid and freeze.

HINT: The sorbet is best eaten within 2–3 days. If it becomes too hard in the freezer, take it out about 15–20 minutes before serving.

To serve

Peel and slice the fruit or wash and hull the berries. Place one or two slices of each fruit around the edge of each plate. Place a scoop of sorbet in the centre of each plate and garnish with a sprig of mint on top.

HINT: Home-made sorbets or ice creams are made without preservatives and emulsifiers and tend to melt around the edges when placed on dishes at room temperatures. To avoid this, place your dishes in the freezer for 5–10 minutes before use.

Sorbet au Piña Colada

POIRES AU VIN ROUGE
Pears in Red Wine

It is always nice to serve a special type of fruit either along with or rather than a rich dessert. These delicately poached pears are very pretty to serve and add a light touch at the end of a dinner.

Cooking time: 30–40 minutes To serve: 6

INGREDIENTS	METRIC	IMPERIAL	AMERICAN
Water	150 ml	5 fl oz	⅔ cup
Red wine (Any type of dry red wine will do, Beaujolais goes very well.)	150 ml	5 fl oz	⅔ cup
Sugar	175 g	6 oz	¾ cup
Strip of lemon rind			
Cinnamon stick	1	1	1
Ripe pears	6	6	6
TO GARNISH:			
Slivered, blanched almonds	15 g	½ oz	1 tbsp

To poach the pears

Place water, wine, sugar, lemon rind, and cinnamon stick in a saucepan large enough to fit the pears snugly. Place over medium heat until the sugar is completely dissolved. Bring to the boil for about 3 minutes. Peel the pears leaving the stems on. Place in the liquid and poach until they are soft. They must poach for at least 30 minutes to ensure that the flavour has reached the middle. During the poaching time turn the pears very gently being careful not to mark them or bruise them. This is best done using the backs of two wooden spoons. When the pears are finished, remove. Take out the lemon strip and cinnamon stick. Boil the liquid until thick and syrupy. Place the pears in a shallow serving bowl and spoon the syrup over them.

To garnish

Toast the almonds on a baking tray in the oven for about 5 minutes until they turn golden and slightly brown on the edges. Be careful not to burn them. Sprinkle over the pears.

To serve

Serve a pear in a fruit dish with some syrup spooned over it.

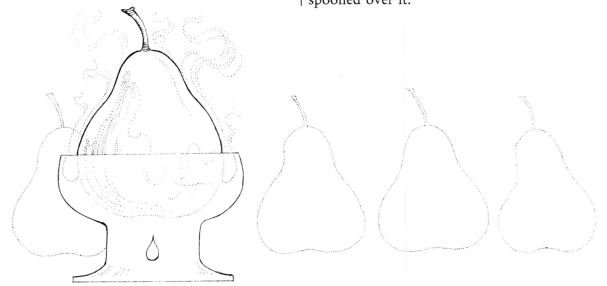

CRÊPES PRALINÉES
Crêpes with Praline Filling

Praline is a blend of nuts and caramelised sugar. It used to be sold ready made in pastry shops. Unfortunately, this is no longer true. In this particular recipe, hazelnuts and almonds are used to make the praline, which is ground to a pulp rather than left crumbly. The crêpes and praline can be made in advance and the crêpes assembled and warmed through before serving.

Cooking time: approximately 35 minutes To serve: 6

INGREDIENTS	METRIC	IMPERIAL	AMERICAN
12 crêpes (page 37)			
FOR THE PRALINE FILLING;			
Castor sugar	175 g	6 oz	¾ cup
Water	85 ml	3 tbsp	3 tbsp
Hazelnuts with skins	75 g	3 oz	¾ cup
Almonds with skins	75 g	3 oz	¾ cup
Almond or peanut oil	7.5 ml	1½ tsp	1½ tsp
Unsalted butter	75 g	3 oz	⅓ cup
Butter	50 g	2 oz	¼ cup
Armagnac or Cognac (good quality brandy)	120 ml	4 fl oz	½ cup
A little oil to oil the baking sheet			

To make the praline
Pre-heat the oven to 180°C/350°F/gas mark 4. Place the hazelnuts and almonds on an ungreased baking sheet and place in the oven to brown. This will take about 5–10 minutes. Be very careful that the nuts do not burn. Oil another baking sheet and set aside. Place the sugar and water in a heavy-bottomed saucepan. Dissolve the sugar over low heat. When the sugar is completely dissolved, bring the liquid to a boil and cook until a caramel or light golden brown colour.

This will take about 5 minutes. Add the roasted nuts and mix well. Quickly pour the mixture onto the oiled baking sheet and let cool. It will easily lift off the sheet when cooled and brittle. Break it up. This can be done in a mortar and pestle or by tapping it in a bowl with the end of a rolling pin. Place in a food processor and process for 1 minute. It will look crumbly.

HINT: Praline will keep in a tightly covered jar for several weeks in the refrigerator and is delicious with ice cream and custards, or in butter creams.

Add the oil and process for 2–3 minutes more, stopping the machine every 20 seconds or so. It should look like a paste and be slightly wet.

To finish
Mix the praline with the butter. Fill each crêpe with a thin layer of praline and fold over.

To serve
Pre-heat the oven to 240°C/475°F/gas mark 9. Put about 50 g/2 oz/¼ cup soft butter on an ovenproof dish and place the crêpes on the butter. Place in the oven for about 30 seconds just to warm the praline through, and melt it slightly. Pour 25 ml/1 tbs armagnac or cognac over each crêpe and serve. Do not flambé.

HINT: The crêpes are best served on individual ovenproof dishes. The sauce is then not lost when the crêpes are moved to the plates.

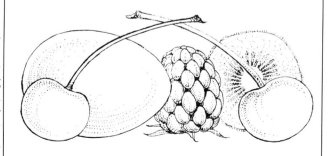

CRÊPES SUZETTES
Orange Flavoured Crêpes

Louis XVI may have been served an early version of these very special crêpes. In addition to the flavouring from the butter and flambé sauce, an almond paste is used to provide a filling that is quite delicious. The crêpes can be made in advance, filled and frozen.

Cooking time: 20 minutes To serve: 6

INGREDIENTS	METRIC	IMPERIAL	AMERICAN
12 crêpes (page 37)			
FOR FILLING:			
Castor sugar	100 g	4 oz	½ cup
Butter	100 g	4 oz	½ cup
Ground almonds	100 g	4 oz	½ cup
Orange liqueur	5 ml	1 tsp	1 tsp
FOR SAUCE:			
Orange liqueur	85 ml	6 tbsp	6 tbsp
Brandy	85 ml	6 tbsp	6 tbsp

HINT: Any type of orange flavoured liqueur may be used. Triple Sec is the least expensive and works well. Otherwise use Cointreau, Grand Marnier, or Curaçao.

To make the filling
Mix the ingredients together with a fork or for a few seconds in a food processor.

HINT: The ground almonds are full of oil and if you mix too strenuously the filling will become oily.

To fill the crêpes
Place the crêpes on a flat surface and put about 10 g/2 tsp of filling on the edge of each one. Roll up the crêpes and place on an ovenproof serving dish. If made ahead, brush the crêpes with melted butter to stop them drying out. The recipe can be made ahead to this point. Either freeze the crêpes until needed (they will keep for several weeks) or refrigerate if only made a short time ahead. Bring to room temperature before placing in the oven.

To finish
Pre-heat the oven to 230°C/450°F/gas mark 8. Place the crêpes in the oven for 5 minutes to warm through. In a separate pan warm the brandy and liqueur.

Crêpes Suzettes

HINT: *If using gas, tip the pan and it will ignite or flambé. If you have electric hobs, throw a lighted match into the warmed alcohol. Remember to remove the match before serving.*

To serve

I find it easier to bring the warm crêpes to the table and flambé the liqueur in a copper pot. I bring the pot to the table and pour the flambé mixture over the crêpes. If you keep stirring the liquid it will continue to flambé. Serve 2 crêpes per person, but plan for seconds!

TARTE AUX POMMES
Apple Tart

Crisp, tart apples are the secret of this most delicious French tart. Once the pastry has been made, all that is left is for the apples to be cut and the tart put together.

Cooking time: 45 minutes To serve: 8

INGREDIENTS	METRIC	IMPERIAL	AMERICAN
Pâte brisée or shortcrust pastry made with 225 g/8 oz flour, to fill 20–23 cm/8–9 in tart tin or flan ring (page 32)			
Apples (Bramley are best. Granny Smith, or Golden Delicious could be substituted)	1.1 kg	2½ lbs	2½ lbs
Castor sugar to sprinkle over top			
Apricot glaze made from half a jar of jam (page 148).			

Pre-heat the oven to 190°C/375°F/gas mark 5.

To prepare the tin
Prepare the pastry and line the tin. Bake the pastry blind for 12 minutes: place greaseproof paper or tissue in tin and fill with dried beans, rice or bread crusts; bake; take out and remove the filling and paper.

To prepare the apples
Peel, core and quarter the apples. Slice evenly and thinly. Save the best slices for the top and fill the pastry shell with the apples. Take the best slices and place them overlapping in a circle around the edge. Make a second circle towards the centre. Take a few slices and arrange them in the shape of a flower in the centre. Generously sprinkle sugar over the top and bake for 45 minutes. The tart should be a golden colour when done.

> *HINT: If the top apples start to burn on the edges during the baking, place a piece of greaseproof paper over the tart so that the heat will not fall on them directly.*

To finish
Take the tart out and remove from the tin. Brush the top with apricot glaze.

TARTE TATIN
Apple Tart with Caramel

The French pastry shops are full of Tartes Tatin in the autumn.

Cooking time: 45 minutes To serve: 8

INGREDIENTS	METRIC	IMPERIAL	AMERICAN
Pâte brisée or shortcrust pastry made with 225 g/8 oz flour (page 32)			
Firm tart apples (Bramley are best, Granny Smith or Golden Delicious will do) approximately	8	8	8
Castor sugar	70 g	2½ oz	¼ cup+ 1 tbsp
Water	50 ml	2 fl oz	¼ cup
Unsalted butter	50 g	2 oz	¼ cup
Lemon zest (grated rind)	1	1	1
Castor sugar	70 g	2½ oz	¼ cup+ 1 tbs
Apricot glaze made from half a jar of jam (page 148)			
Pie plate or fixed bottom tart tin 20–23 cm/8–9 in			

To prepare the caramel
Dissolve the 70 g/2½ oz sugar in water. When the sugar is completely dissolved, bring the water to a boil. Do not boil before all the sugar is dissolved. Bring to a caramel or light brown colour. Pour immediately into the tart tin or pie plate and rotate the plate so that the caramel will completely cover the bottom. Leave to harden.

To fill the tin
Peel, core and slice the apples. Melt the butter in a large saucepan. Add the lemon zest and

sugar to dissolve. Add the apple slices and sauté 2–3 minutes. Be careful not to break the slices. Pour into a baking sheet to cool.

Select the nicest looking slices and arrange them overlapping on the bottom of the tin. Remember that the dish will be presented upside-down so the rounded edges of the apples should be hidden from you. Continue to arrange in circles until the bottom is covered. Completely fill the cavity with the remaining apples.

Prepare the pastry. Roll out the pastry and place over the top of the apples. Prick with a fork.

To bake

Pre-heat the oven to 200°C/400°F/gas mark 6. Place the tart on a baking sheet and put it in the centre of the oven.

HINT: The oven should be at temperature before the tart goes in to set the pastry.

Bake for 45 minutes. Remove from the oven and run a knife around the edges to loosen the crust. Let the pie rest for 5 minutes. Turn it upside-down onto a round serving platter. Brush the top with apricot glaze.

HINT: If the tart is allowed to rest too long before turning out, the caramel will harden and it will be difficult to turn out.

PÂTE SUCRÉE
Sweet Tart Pastry

Dessert tarts are enhanced by this sweet, biscuit-type pastry. It is a much easier dough to handle than shortcrust pastry. It can be re-rolled and re-shaped without spoiling the quality. It's a good idea to have tart shells baked and frozen during the spring and summer fruit season. You can then easily put together a delicious tart.

Cooking time: 15–20 minutes To serve: 6–8

INGREDIENTS	METRIC	IMPERIAL	AMERICAN
To fill 15–18 cm/8–10 in tart ring or tin:			
Plain flour	225 g	8 oz	1 cup
Pinch of salt			
Unsalted butter, softened	100 g	4 oz	½ cup
Castor sugar	100 g	4 oz	½ cup
Egg yolks	4	4	4

4 drops vanilla extract (if unavailable use vanilla sugar instead of castor sugar)

Sift flour and salt together onto a working surface. Make a wide circle with a hole in the centre. Place the softened butter in the middle. With your fingers make a neat little nest in the centre of the butter. Put the sugar on top, the egg yolks on this and the vanilla on top of the yolks. Using your fingers and a tapping motion, work the mixture until it is smooth being careful not to let it touch the flour. Making a large centre hole will help here. When the mixture is smooth, draw in the flour and work until it comes together in a ball. Try not to let the dough touch the palm of your hand which is the warmest part of the hand. Chill at least 1 hour or overnight.

HINT: This is a rich, soft dough. If it is not very cold when you roll it out then you may have difficulty.

Roll out the pastry and line your tin. If baking blind, pre-heat the oven to 190°C/375°F/gas mark 5. Place some tissue or greaseproof paper in the tin and fill with rice, dried beans, or bread crusts to weigh down the paper. Place in the oven. After 12 minutes take out and remove the false filling and paper. Place back in the oven to finish baking. It should be a light golden colour, which will take about another 3–8 minutes depending on the size of the tart.

TARTE AUX POIRES
Pear Tart

The sweet tart pastry combined with a light custard and ripe pears make this one of my family's favourite treats. It is a welcome change from the usual winter fruit tarts. The pastry may be made ahead and frozen uncooked.

Cooking time: 45 minutes To serve: 8

INGREDIENTS	METRIC	IMPERIAL	AMERICAN
One 20 cm/8 in tart tin lined with pâte sucrée (see page 146)			
Double (heavy) cream	150 ml	5 fl oz	¾ cup
Eggs	2	2	2
Castor sugar	40 g	1½ oz	3 tbsp
Ripe pears	5	5	5

Pre-heat the oven to 190°C/375°F/gas mark 5
Mix the cream, eggs, and sugar in a bowl.
Peel the pears and slice in half lengthwise. Remove the core and stem. Place the pear on a cutting surface flat side down. Slice the pear vertically to form narrow half circles, leaving the slices in order so the pear retains its shape. Carefully lift the pear into the lined tart with the round end near the edge and the narrow end pointing towards the middle. Quickly prepare the other pears in this manner. To fill the middle, cut the narrow end off one pear half and place the rounded ball, sliced in the same way, in the centre. Pour the cream mixture over the pears to fill the tart, and place it in the oven.

Bake for about half an hour and check to see if the pie is browning too quickly on top. If it is, place a piece of greaseproof paper over it. Bake until the custard is set, usually no more than 45 minutes in all. It is done when a knife inserted in the custard comes out clean. It should be a very light golden colour. Cool.

To finish
Glaze the top.

Glaze
Use a glaze to seal and give an extra shine or professional looking finish to your tarts. For light fruit use apricot jam. For dark or red fruit use redcurrant jam.

INGREDIENTS	METRIC	IMPERIAL	AMERICAN
Jam	75 g	6 tbsp	6 tbsp
Water	50 ml	2 tbsp	2 tbsp
Squeeze of lemon			

Heat the jam, water and lemon juice in a heavy-bottomed saucepan without boiling or stirring. Boiling will make the glaze look muddy. When it is liquid strain through a wire sieve.

HINT: I find it easiest to make an entire jar of jam into a glaze and store the glaze in the jar. It will keep several weeks in the refrigerator. It can be taken out and re-warmed any number of times. When needed, I simply heat whatever is necessary. Try not to boil it when heating; it will begin to caramelise.

To spread
The best result is achieved by dabbing the glaze on while it is very hot. Brush it on gently starting in the centre and working outward. Try not to go back over areas already covered.

To serve
Bring to the table, slice and serve.

TARTE AUX FRAISES
Strawberry Tart

The arrival of strawberry tarts in the pastry shop windows heralds the coming of spring. Make the pastry in advance and freeze and you can then put together tarts as good as those in pâtisseries in only a few minutes.

Cooking time: 15–20 minutes To serve: 8

INGREDIENTS	METRIC	IMPERIAL	AMERICAN
One 20 cm/8 in pâte sucrée case, baked (page 146).			
FOR CRÈME PÂTISSIÈRE:			
Egg yolks	5	5	5
Castor sugar	175 g	6 oz	¾ cup
Corn flour	70 g	2¾ oz	¼ cup+ 1 tbsp
Vanilla pod	1	1	1
Milk	425 g	15 fl oz	2 cup
Unsalted butter	15 g	½ oz	1 tbsp
FOR TOPPING			
Strawberries	680 g	1½ lb	1½ lb
Glaze made with redcurrant jelly (page 148)			

To make the crème pâtissière
Beat the egg yolks with a rotary or electric beater and slowly add the sugar. Continue to beat until the mixture is nearly white and begins to form a ribbon. Lift the beaters and form a W. If this remains, the ribbon stage has been reached. Beat in the corn flour.

Place the vanilla pod in the milk and bring to the boil. Remove the pod. While still beating the eggs, slowly pour in the milk.

Pour the mixture into a saucepan and place over a moderate heat, stirring constantly. The sauce will become lumpy as it comes to the boil. Do not worry. The flour prevents curdling and the mixture will become smooth as you stir.

Beat over the heat for a few minutes to cook the flour. Remove from the heat and stir in the butter. If you are not going to use it immediately, place a piece of buttered greaseproof paper over the top to prevent a skin from forming. It will keep for a few days in the refrigerator or can be frozen.

To assemble the tart
Wash, stem and hull the strawberries. Place the baked pastry shell on a serving dish and spread a layer of the crème pâtissière on the bottom. Carefully place the strawberries on this base, stem side down. To make them look uniform slice off the hull end of the larger ones so that they are all the same height. Warm the glaze and brush over the strawberries. The tart should be served on the same day.

HINT: For a lighter touch or a faster result, use sweetened whipped cream as a base rather than a crème pâtissière.

To serve
Slice and serve.

GÂTEAU LÉGER AU CHOCOLAT
Special Chocolate Cake

Making this cake requires only a very small amount of potato flour which produces a light texture and allows the chocolate flavour to be predominant. It is a rich and moist cake that tastes better made one day in advance.

Cooking time: 45 minutes To serve: 8

INGREDIENTS	METRIC	IMPERIAL	AMERICAN
Semi-sweet chocolate	200 g	7 oz	7 oz
Instant coffee	25 ml	2 tbsp	2 tbsp
Water	40 ml	3 tbsp	3 tbsp
Eggs, separated	4	4	4
Unsalted butter, room temperature	140 g	5 oz	½ cup+1 tbsp
Pinch of salt			
Castor sugar	100 g	4 oz	½ cup
Potato starch (corn flour may be substituted)	50 g	2 oz	¼ cup
FOR DECORATION:			
Double (heavy) cream	150 ml	5 oz	⅔ cup
Icing (confectioner's) sugar	25 g	2 tbsp	2 tbsp
Chopped walnuts or praline	175 g	6 oz	1 cup
Cake tin 23 cm/9 in (a moule-à-manque works well here)			

Pre-heat the oven to 180°C/350°F/gas mark 4

To prepare the cake tin

Cut a piece of greaseproof paper to fit the bottom of the tin. Melt some fat and brush the bottom of the tin. Place the paper in the tin and brush the paper and sides of the tin with fat. Sprinkle the sides and bottom with castor sugar and the bottom with a small amount of flour. Shake out the excess.

To make the cake

Melt the chocolate, coffee and water in a heavy-bottomed pan over a low heat. There is less chance of the chocolate burning if you place the pan in a bain Marie or in another pan of hot water. Stir frequently.

HINT: Keep the heat low or work over water. If the heat is too high, the cocoa fats will separate and you will not have a smooth mixture.

When the chocolate is melted, take off the heat and add the egg yolks one at a time.

HINT: You are incorporating one fat into another, and if you add one too fast you will have a curdling effect similar to that which occurs when making mayonnaise. If this does happen, beat the mixture with an electric beater or put in a food processor. The chocolate should become smooth.

Remove from the heat and add the butter in pieces, mixing well before the next piece is added. Stir until smooth.

Beat the whites with the salt to a medium peak. The peaks will form but not be firm. Sprinkle on the sugar and carefully beat to form stiff peaks. Beat in the potato starch. Take a spoonful of the whites and mix into the cooled chocolate to lighten it. Fold the chocolate into the whites and turn into the prepared tin.

To bake

Bake in the middle of your oven for 40–45 minutes. Remove the tin to a cake rack and cool for 1 hour. The cake will be slightly creamy and puffed up when it comes out of the oven. While it cools, it will deflate and crack slightly. Slide a palette knife between the sides of the tin and the cake and turn out onto a cake rack to finish cooling.

To decorate

Whip the cream with the sugar. When the cake has completely cooled, spread a thin layer of the cream around the sides being careful not to get any on the top. Take the chopped walnuts or praline in your hand and gently press them into the cream working all around the sides. Place the cream in a piping bag and make 5 rosettes on the top.

HINT: If you prefer, omit the rosettes and simply sprinkle icing sugar on the top just before serving.

To serve

Keep the cake in the refrigerator until 30 minutes before serving. Slice and serve.

CHOCOLAT PRALINÉ AVEC CHANTILLY
Chocolate with Praline and Whipped Cream

This is like a great big chocolate truffle filled with praline and decorated with whipped cream. For those of you who are chocaholics, there is nothing better. It is a rich, chocolate dessert that defies description. It is essential to buy the best chocolate available to attain the desired result.

Cooking time: 20 minutes To serve: 6–8

INGREDIENTS	METRIC	IMPERIAL	AMERICAN
FOR PRALINE:			
Almonds with skins	75 g	3 oz	¾ cup
Castor sugar	75 g	3 oz	¾ cup
FOR CHOCOLATE:			
Semi-sweet chocolate	340 g	12 oz	¾ lb
Water	120 ml	4 fl oz	½ cup
Unsalted butter	75 g	3 oz	⅓ cup
Double (heavy) cream	225 ml	8 fl oz	1 cup
Rum or brandy	50 ml	2 tbsp	¼ cup
TO GARNISH:			
Double (heavy) cream	225 ml	8 fl oz	1 cup
Round chocolate after dinner mints: about 10			
A bomb shaped mould. (This is a pretty way to serve this dessert as the sides are completely straight. However, a small pudding basin or rectangular loaf tin is fine.)			
A little oil to oil the mould.			

Lightly oil the mould.
To make the praline
Oil a baking sheet and set aside. Place the sugar and almonds in a small heavy-bottomed pan. Slowly melt the sugar and wait for it to become a caramel colour. As soon as it reaches this colour pour it onto the baking sheet.

HINT: The sugar should melt and cook to a light brown colour. At the same time the almonds will cook in the sugar and you will hear a slight popping noise as they do. Be careful not to touch the caramel as it can give a nasty burn.

Set in a cool spot to harden. This will take 10–15 minutes. When it is hard, it will easily lift off the sheet in one piece. Break it up in a mortar and pestle or by tapping it in a bowl with the end of a rolling pin. Place in a food processor and grind to small pieces. This can also be done in a cheese mill or liquidiser. (The praline will keep for several weeks in a tightly closed jar in a cool dry place. It is delicious over ice cream, as a cake decoration or in fillings.)
To make the chocolate cream
Melt the chocolate and water in a saucepan until it is a thick cream. There is less chance of the chocolate burning if you place the pan in a bain Marie or in another pan of hot water.

Cream the butter and add to the cooled chocolate. Beat in the praline and add the rum. Half whip the cream so that it is the same consistency as the chocolate. Be sure the chocolate is cooled and fold in the cream. Turn into the mould and cover with cling film. Refrigerate until firm. Let it set at least 3 hours or overnight.
To finish
Remove the mould from the refrigerator about 15 minutes before unmoulding. Dip the bottom of the mould in hot water to free the chocolate cream. Slip a knife around the edges and turn out onto a serving plate. Whip the cream and make large rosettes all around the base. Place the mints standing up in the cream at approximately 5 cm/2 in intervals. The dish can be kept in the refrigerator until ready to serve or it can be frozen without the cream decoration.
To serve
Slice as a cake in small pieces as it is rich.

Chocolat Praliné avec Chantilly

GRIESTORTE AUX FRAISES

Griestorte with Strawberries

A light touch for any meal is provided by this Alsatian cake with a lemony flavour. It is made with semolina instead of plain flour. This gives the cake a crunchy texture that blends well with the strawberries and cream.

Cooking time: 45 minutes To serve: 6

INGREDIENTS	METRIC	IMPERIAL	AMERICAN
Eggs, separated	3	3	3
Castor sugar	125 g	4½ oz	½ cup+ 1 tbsp
Zest and juice of ½ lemon			
Fine semolina	75 g	3 oz	⅓ cup
Ground almonds	25 g	1 oz	2 tbsp
FOR FILLING:			
Double (heavy) cream	150 ml	5 oz	⅔ cup
Castor sugar	15 g	1 tbsp	1 tbsp
Strawberries	225 g	8 oz	2 cups
Icing (confectioner's) sugar for sprinkling			

Moule-à-manque: 18 cm/7 in (This is a French term for a round tin that has sloping sides. Thus, when the cake is turned out the base will be wider than the top. Any shaped tin may be used, square or round. The mixture should three quarters fill the tin).

Pre-heat the oven to 180°C/350°F/gas mark 4

To prepare the cake tin

Cut a piece of greaseproof paper to fit the bottom of the tin.

Melt some fat and brush the bottom of the tin with it. Place the paper in the bottom and grease the paper. Brush the sides with the fat. Sprinkle castor sugar all around the inside of the tin. Sprinkle a small amount of flour in the bottom. Shake out any excess. Set aside.

HINT: This method ensures that your cake will easily pop out of the tin without leaving the bottom part behind.

To make the cake

Cream the egg yolks and sugar together until they become thick and are actually white. This can take 5–10 minutes in an electric mixer. The eggs are the only leavening agent and should be well worked. Add the zest or lemon skin to the mixture and continue to cream. Add the lemon juice little by little. Stir in the semolina and almonds. Let it rest for 10 minutes. The semolina needs this time to absorb the moisture and expand.

Whisk the egg whites to a medium peak. (This means whisk until the mixture will stand in soft peaks as opposed to firm ones.) Take a spoonful of whites and mix into the egg yolk mixture to lighten it. Then fold the yolk mixture into the whites.

Pour into the prepared cake tin and bake in the centre of your oven for 40–45 minutes. The cake is done when a knife inserted comes out clean and the sides have begun to shrink away from the tin. Take out of the oven and run a knife around the edges of the tin. Turn out onto a cake rack. Let cool. It may be prepared ahead to this point and stored in a cake tin for up to one day, or frozen.

To garnish

Cut the cake in half to make a top and bottom layer. Whip the cream with the sugar to sweeten. Wash and hull the strawberries and dry thoroughly. Spread the centre of the cake with the cream. Cut the strawberries in half and place on the cream. Put the top half back on the strawberries. Sprinkle icing sugar on the top.

To serve

Bring to the table, slice and serve.

HINT: If the strawberries are not sweet, sprinkle some sugar over them before placing in the cake. Other fruits may be used.

LE GÂTEAU SEVILLAN
Orange Cake

A French cake is usually made by first weighing the eggs and then weighing all of the other ingredients to match. Thus, you will notice in this cake that the flour, sugar and butter are equal amounts. This recipe makes a lovely dessert and is also perfect for a luncheon or tea. It's light, full of flavour and always a success.

Cooking time: 30 minutes To serve: 6

INGREDIENTS	METRIC	IMPERIAL	AMERICAN
Butter	100 g	4 oz	½ cup
Castor sugar	100 g	4 oz	½ cup
Eggs, size 2	2	2	2
Plain flour	100 g	4 oz	½ cup
Baking powder	5 g	1 tsp	1 tsp
Juice and zest (grated skin) of orange	1	1	1
Icing (confectioner's) sugar	100 g	4 oz	½ cup
Icing (confectioner's) sugar for sprinkling			
Sandwich tin: 5 cm/6 in			

Pre-heat oven to 190°C/375°F/gas mark 5

To prepare the cake tin
Cut a piece of greaseproof paper to fit the bottom of the tin. Melt some fat and brush the bottom of the tin with it. Place the paper in the bottom and grease the paper. Brush the sides of the tin with the fat. Sprinkle castor sugar all around the inside of the tin. Sprinkle a small amount of flour in the bottom. Shake out any excess. Set aside.

To make the cake
Cream the butter in an electric mixer or by hand and add the sugar little by little. Work the mixture until it becomes white. Add the eggs one at a time.

HINT: If the eggs are added too quickly, the mixture will curdle and you will not have as light a cake. I break up the eggs in a separate bowl and slowly pour them in while beating.

Sift in the flour and baking powder. Add the zest to the mixture. Turn into the cake tin and bake for 30 minutes. It is done when the cake shrinks away from the sides of the tin and a knife inserted in the centre comes out clean. Run a knife around the edge of the tin and turn the cake out onto a cake rack.

To make the syrup
Mix the orange juice and icing sugar together until smooth. Carefully spoon the syrup over the top of the cake so that it absorbs all of the liquid. This should be done while the cake is warm.

To serve
Sprinkle the top of the cooled cake with icing sugar and serve in slices.

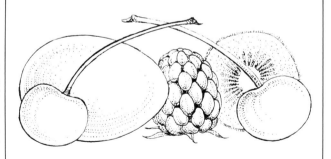

BRIOCHE AU CHOCOLAT
Brioche with Chocolate Cream

The sweet brioche dough makes a wonderful shell for this smooth chocolate filling. Either make your own brioche (page 31) or buy one large or several small individual ones. This is a different way to serve brioche and your guests will enjoy the mixture of flavours.

Cooking time: 10 minutes To serve: 6

INGREDIENTS	METRIC	IMPERIAL	AMERICAN
Semi-sweet chocolate	140 g	5 oz	5 oz
Water	40 ml	3 tbsp	3 tbsp
Milk	3 ml	10 fl oz	1¼ cups
Plain flour	25 g	2 tbsp	2 tbsp
Eggs	2	2	2
Sugar	25 g	2 tbsp	2 tbsp
Double (heavy) cream	25 ml	2 tbsp	2 tbsp
1 large round brioche or 6 small ones (page 31)			

To make the chocolate cream
Place the chocolate and water into a saucepan and heat on a low heat to melt. There is less chance of the chocolate burning if you place the pan in a bain Marie or in another pan of hot water.

When the chocolate is smooth, whisk in the milk. Beat the flour, eggs, and sugar until well blended. Add the melted chocolate to the egg mixture stirring constantly. Place back on the heat and beat until thick. It will become lumpy before it goes smooth. Do not worry, the flour prevents curdling and it will smooth as you beat. Cook for several minutes to cook the flour. Take off the heat and continue to stir until it cools; Add the cream when it is cool.

To assemble
Slice off the top of the brioche and hollow out the centre leaving about 2.5 cm to 4 cm/1 to 1½ in around the edges. Fill the inside with the cooled chocolate. Replace the top making sure some of the chocolate is showing.

To serve
Place on a serving dish and slice like a cake. Or serve the individual brioche on separate plates.

HINT: This filling may be used in many varying ways, for example: to fill the centre of cakes or choux pastry. It will keep several days in the refrigerator or may be frozen.

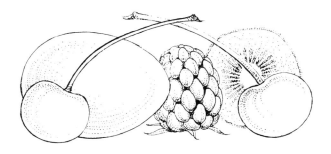

Brioche au Chocolat

INDEX